the Death
of Tinker Bell

the Death of Tinker Bell

the American Theatre
in the 20th Century

JOSEPH GOLDEN

SYRACUSE UNIVERSITY PRESS

for David and Dan
who are still on intimate
terms with Tinker Bell

ACKNOWLEDGMENTS

The brief excerpts from Tennessee Williams' THE NIGHT OF THE IGUANA (copyright 1961 by Two Rivers Enterprises, Inc.); I RISE IN FLAME, CRIED THE PHOENIX (copyright 1951 by Tennessee Williams); and "Person-to-Person," the Preface to CAT ON A HOT TIN ROOF (copyright 1955 by Tennessee Williams) are reprinted by permission of the publisher, New Directions Publishing Corporation.

The excerpt from VICTIMS OF DUTY by Eugène Ionesco, translated by Donald Watson, published by Grove Press, Inc. (copyright 1958 by John Calder [Publishers] Limited) is reprinted by permission of Grove Press, Inc.

Lines from ARIA DA CAPO, Harper & Row. Copyright 1920, 1947 by Edna St. Vincent Millay. By permission of Norma Millay Ellis.

The excerpt from Brooks Atkinson's "His Bizarre Images Can't Be Denied," © 1961 by the New York Times Company. Reprinted by permission.

The excerpts from Archibald MacLeish's THE FALL OF THE CITY and J. B. are reprinted by permission of the publisher, Houghton Mifflin Company.

Robert Corrigan's remarks are from his essay, "The Theater in Search of a 'Fix,' " which appears in *Theatre in the 20th Century*, published by Grove Press, edited by Mr. Corrigan. Reprinted by permission of the author.

The excerpt from Eugene O'Neill's LONG DAY'S JOURNEY INTO NIGHT is reprinted by permission of Carlotta Monterey O'Neill and Yale University Press. Copyright © 1955 by Carlotta Monterey O'Neill.

OUR TOWN and THE SKIN OF OUR TEETH by Thornton Wilder are published by Harper & Row, Inc.

Excerpts from *American Drama*, by Louis Broussard. Copyright 1962 by the University of Oklahoma Press. Reprinted by permission of the publisher.

Preface

It is the purpose of this informal, yet serious, book to recreate something of the cultural and philosophical climate in which the American theatre operates today. In a sense, these essays represent a "primer" on the imperatives of theatrical life in the 20th century, as well as a review of those artists, critics, and thinkers who seem to best embody these imperatives. The essays are addressed to a special audience, that vast middle band on the spectrum of American cultural life, who are neither the professional makers of theatre nor its professional critics or teachers. Rather, an audience that is attuned, by virtue of education and personal interest, to the special pleasure the theatre can offer, but who, for occupational reasons, lack the opportunity to draw together the critical theory and opinion that most influence the practice of theatre today. These essays reflect a strong personal bias, to be sure, but they also include commentary by those observers who have been most instrumental in defining the intellectual and emotional state of the theatre. In other words, *The Death of Tinker Bell* is a point of view as well as an effort to sharpen the sensibilities of the playgoing public.

I wish to extend special thanks to Mr. Tom Cummings of the Syracuse University College Humanistic Studies Center, who lured *Tinker Bell,* in the form of my six public lectures that served as a basis for this book, into existence; to Mr. Richard Wilson of the Syracuse University News Bureau, whose steadfast encouragement kept my morale alive at critical moments; and to my wife, Fay, who offered the ultimate support by listening. . . .

JOSEPH GOLDEN

Syracuse, New York
August, 1966

Contents

Contents

i

The Death of Tinker Bell

To discuss the death of anything—even so whimsical a piece of fiction as Peter Pan's friend Tinker Bell—tends to lend a stern and somber atmosphere to any discussion. Rather like a requiem, in fact. The mood darkens when you realize—as you will shortly—that it's my intention to conduct something of an autopsy on the remains. It will darken even further when you learn that it will be a semiphilosophic autopsy, born of unavoidably strong prejudices and personal convictions.

The tone will be mostly negative—but not for negative purposes. Usually, it's fun to be negative; it attracts attention, it's almost fashionable, because then you don't risk being accused of naïve optimism in a wholly pessimistic age. But I'm not out for this kind of easy fun or that kind of grim fashion. You see, I love the theatre. I love it unashamedly, even at the risk of sounding maudlin, in all its primitive, lofty, and absurd attitudes. I love it not because it is old, but because it is new. Not because it is "important," but because it is necessary. Not because it provides escape, but because it demands reentry. I am in awe of the theatre's original objectives: to bridge the gulf between the limitless and almost incomprehensible designs of life and the peculiarly small and insular role man is obliged to play in it;

to bring him into a confrontation with himself so that he may better judge his capacity for living in harmony with himself (the microcosm) and the total universe (the macrocosm); to preserve, in living images, a few of those elusive truths about his life and render them, if only briefly, into memorable and beautiful forms. I make no apology for the abstract and ecstatic sound to these objectives. They were true a million years ago when—as Robert Edmond Jones imagines it—Ook, Pung, and Little Zowie re-created the dangers and triumphs of the daily hunt of the great Sabre-Tooth by way of proving that man was equal to the hostile world that surrounded him. These objectives are no less true—and necessary—today. I apologize only for the *lack* of people who believe in and live by them. My profound affection for the theatre—and bear in mind that I'm referring to an artistic concept and not a place where plays are given—will, I suspect, seem in grave doubt as we proceed. But please don't forget it; it will have to sustain us as we make this excursion through the immortal remains of Tinker Bell.

There is, I suppose, something undeniably facetious in adopting the name of Barrie's fanciful little blip of uninhibited light for a serious examination of the theatre. There is something undeniably sentimental as well, when we recall how we may have been tempted to join our children in the furious clapping of hands when Peter Pan asks our help in saving Tinker Bell from extinction.

We really needn't be ashamed of the fancy or the sentiment, nor of aligning ourselves with our children's interest. We aren't so sophisticated that we have forgotten what a creature like Tinker Bell represents to us—or once did. We haven't become *that* immune to the taste for utter freedom, for the joy of defying time and space, for the delight in altering our vision of the world around us, for awe, wonder, and magic. We are a little out of practice, perhaps; a little reluctant to believe that we might still manage to enjoy the *possibilities,* rather than merely the necessities of living.

Not as an escape mechanism, mind you. Gin and vermouth require considerably less effort. But rather as a willing engagement with those poorly contained and continually nagging memories—more often called human myths—inherited at birth that threaten to pull us off our civilized plateaus. These myths—whether they deal with death or love or God, or the unpredictable drifts of man's nature—are the collective experience that grows out of the psychic and spiritual needs and energies of a race, a culture, a nation. These needs become embodied in permanent, highly formal acts we call ritual, and serve, ultimately, as the fountainhead of great literature, religious and secular thought, art, and music. And why? Because myth, like art, is the distillation, the purification of random and weakly perceived experience, rendering it into those stark and universal terms that awaken the common fund of inborn memory. If, then, Tinker Bell symbolizes this kind of myth, this reawakening of our half-forgotten potential for sharing universal dreams and experiences, then the American theatre has been woefully negligent in keeping Tinker Bell alive. Before attempting to outline how, when, and why the American theatre has so gratuitously dealt death blows, please indulge me while I do some innocent speculating.

I confess to some strong views on the theatre: what it is, how it came to be, what it's meant to accomplish. Please note that I don't claim they are *original* views, only strong, and that they are bound to color any subsequent observations. These views should be ordinary, coin-of-the-realm views, garden-variety views, household words of the theatre. The fact that they're not can easily result in my being cast as the innocent lamb, the professorial ostrich—with his ideas and ideals buried in academic sand.

But I don't mind. I have good companions in the sand

with me: Michel St. Denis, Henri Gheon, Stark Young, Robert Edmond Jones, Antonin Artaud, Gordon Craig, Eric Bentley and a dozen or so other men who have behaved and spoken with a singular purpose in mind: to reforge the link that binds the theatre irrevocably to life and to use the instruments of the stage to make vivid those perceptions of human experience that might otherwise escape us.

The theatre, you see, is a humanity. As such, its goal has been, despite frequent deviations, to celebrate man's capacity both to endure and to control the universe that constantly threatens to engulf him. The grandeur of an Oedipus, an Antigone, a Hamlet—even a Willy Loman, doesn't lie in the emotional dimensions of the character, in the glorious language they are obliged to mouth, or in the fierce encounters they have with their visible enemies. Character, language, and contest are very nice; they keep an audience from getting bored. But the ultimate source of power in an Oedipus or a Hamlet lies in the deep knowledge they possess that they are engaged in one of those cataclysmic conflicts with universal questions of justice and honor, questions which they dare to challenge, and answer with their lives if necessary, in order to bring a discordant universe back into some form of harmony. This is an awesome business, especially when we consider that although characters, language, and contests may be different, the questions today are unchanged, despite the evasive tactics used by walking "Barefoot in the Park," by falling in "Luv," or listening to the hoots and the meows of "The Owl and the Pussycat."

Ivory tower, academic, unrealistic thinking? Out of touch with the facts and imperatives of the contemporary legitimate theatre? A faintly smug professorial view of the besmirched commercial stage? Possibly so. But hardly worse than the rampant cynicism, the intellectual exhaustion, the cannibal-like ethic that rules much of the legitimate stage at present. If the vision that man can still be equal, if not superior, to the real world is one of two evil choices, I prefer such a choice. And I prefer to think that the theatre, with its living metaphors of human need and action, with its totally plastic and graphic evocations of human tension and conflict, and with its infinite capacity for transforming the most complex philosophic and moral reflections into highly charged, profoundly emotional recognitions, continues to preserve its potential as one of the foremost tenets of the humanist tradition.

And as a humanity, it touches us, directly—where we live. When the theatre is truly great, when it awakens in us the dimly remembered dreams of our potential for love, for honesty, for courage, for profound compassion—even, indeed, for profound hatred—it ennobles all of us.

The theatre as a humanity, as a crucible for the most intellectual cerebration as well as for the most raw and primitive feelings, is a proper, healthy home for Tinker Bell. But the promise and stability of this home has been demoralized in American theatre by four conditions: (1) the peculiar vulnerabilities of the theatre itself; (2) the destructive economic situation of the theatre; (3) the traditional American hostility toward serious drama; and (4) the peculiarities of contemporary social and moral attitudes.

One might think it was hard to erode and demoralize so venerable, universal, and respected an institution as the theatre. Yet it's really quite easy. The theatre, like the human beings it serves as aesthetic agent and commentator, is possessed of the same sort of strengths and frailties that human beings possess. This humanoid character of the theatre is, of course, its greatest source of power, its means of establishing a kinship, a bond of familiarity and compassion between the stage and the spectator that no other art form can accomplish—or, for that matter, *wants* to accomplish. In watching a play, an audience will search for itself, for those habits, customs, quirks, little self-deceptions, grand and heroic gestures, and those passionate aches that identify the fear, love, or hatred the audience itself has experienced. The theatre is compulsive about this, to the extent of urging the audience to abrogate its intellectual, critical judgments, so that it *feels* rather than thinks its way through a play. Ironical, isn't it? To arrive at a great, stunning, truthful revelation about man's relationship to himself is to precipitate great *thought*. Yet the catalyst is great emotion. Not so ironical after all. For the great hold the theatre enjoys is its capacity to reflect on and to employ skillfully the most elemental conflicts known to man: the struggle between his brain and his body, between light and dark, between good and evil. And to embody this struggle in those acts and symbols that are drawn from the deepest reservoir of human memory and experience is surely one of the most compelling features of the living theatre. Ideally, man ought to feel utterly "at home" in the theatre. But too often he doesn't; indeed, he frequently feels a little alien, remote, and insulated from the exclusive experience being developed up on the stage.

The theatre often pays a heavy penalty for this commitment to reality. Because it must re-create credible images of man engaged in dramatic affairs, affairs that are themselves accurately described and motivated, and that result in a complete and satisfying conclusion, the theatre is vulnerable to the accusation of seeming *artless,* relatively "easy," and thus not to be taken too seriously. Painting, music, and sculpture are taken seriously—too seriously sometimes. But not the theatre. Perhaps one reason is that the audience has lost just enough faith in its own capacity to make penetrating critical and emotional judgments and is embarrassed when it tries to take *itself* seriously. Or perhaps because the theatre continues to try to make audiences believe that they're not watching theatre at all, but the "real thing," thus denying itself its own special identity, something that painting, music, and sculpture rarely do.

A major source of the theatre's vulnerability is the fact that it is a temporal art. It exists in time. It must be projected and captured *at the moment it happens,* and no other. Because our normal conception of time is radically altered in the theatre (three days, three weeks, three centuries may be asked to pass in two hours) the values a play offers must be imbedded into the consciousness of an audience with terrific force, requiring that all the vocal and mimetic activity be rendered starkly and vividly, so that the imprint is made. Sound vibrates only a few seconds, and is lost. The significant trembling of a hand is brusquely wiped away in fragments of seconds to give way to another piece of "business." In the theatre, the needle cannot be lifted and dropped back fifteen grooves. A play moves forward immutably, depending, at least in part, on the momentum it gathers as it goes, forcing the spectators to abandon their usual preoccupation with clock hours in favor of a heightened sense of movement that lends compression and urgency to the action.

This compression and urgency is unusually easy to destroy. A momentary distraction, the inept handling of a prop, the poorly articulated word, the fuzzy composition of bodies that fails to direct interest and attention, the lighting effect that bumps up too fast—and the audience becomes instinctively aware of the ticking on their wrists instead of the emotional pulse on the stage. It's very sad, but very true: being committed to the revelations of the flesh, the theatre must suffer the inadequacies of the flesh. (Which begins to explain, in part, why so many major theoreticians of the stage preferred puppets and marionettes.) The theatre's effects, then, are transient. Which is good, because so is life and the theatre can isolate its critical moments; which is bad, because, being transient and climactic in intention, the theatre risks comprehension, and thus interest, and thus importance, and thus seriousness of purpose.

The theatre, we also know, is a highly *conventional* medium; that is, it depends on a *convening,* a coming together of audience and play, a kind of tacit agreement, a bargain struck between players and play-watchers which runs something like: "I know," the spectator says, "that what you're doing is illusory, is essentially make-believe. But I also know that you're trying to use the illusion and make-believe to make me conscious of some dimension of my life that I have missed myself. So . . . I will *accept the lie,* the premise on which you're operating, the fiction. If you agree to sustain and be utterly true and consistent to the kind of myth you plan to weave up there, I agree to *suspend my disbelief*—and we'll get along fine." All well and good; provided the production *can* be true to and sustain the myth; that there are no obstacles—imperfect perceptions on the part of both player and viewer about what constitutes the external manifestations of the play's style. The convention will work and will fulfill its essential task— that of removing the barriers that obstruct mutual understanding—if the truce line is respected and there are no violations on either side; if playwrights, for instance, as they unfold their dramatic speculations, refrain from becoming coy or cute, ambiguous or myopic, self-conscious or pontifical, sacred or philosophical and thereby skew the function of theatre toward an entirely private and arbitrary area; if actors concentrate on acting the *play* and not displaying themselves and thus introduce conventions of egomania that are antithetical to the *gestalt,* the total picture, the singular, enduring metaphor of human experience the play may be trying to formulate; if the audience actively works to open its emotional pores and absorb the play and not indulge in discursive speculation about the notorious romances of the leading lady, or the crisis of baby-sitting out in Hempstead, or the calamities of the rising crush of interoffice memos.

Conventions change, of course, as both the level and kind of expectations about life change. What never changes, however, is the fragility, the tenuousness that exists once the bargain is struck and the uncommon ease with which one partner or the other can default on the deal. Once the defaulting is committed the play is in peril, and so is the theatre.

One final peculiarity that makes the theatre both strong and deeply vulnerable: it is a symbolic art. Symbols are potent things. When they are well conceived and well wrought, they contain resonances and implications that always threaten to erupt through the thin skin of language and physical action used to convey them. Because of the enormous obligation of any art form to select, compress, and refine symbols in the hope that the art work will carry the maximum emotional and intellectual freight, they *become the statement of life itself,* not merely the pathway to it. And anything preposterous enough to claim to be a highly concentrated "statement of life," to claim that a disemboweled cow, or suspended toilet seats, or a pink lampshade, will carry the freight without derailing the train is on a very hazardous journey.

It's one of the abiding paradoxes in the theatre that a play should be a truthful image of life while at the same time condensing and modifying life into evocative, symbolic tokens. All very well and all very basic to the function of any artist. But both the temporal and conventional nature of the theatre, plus its implicit promise to keep faith with the communal experience of a wide and diverse audience, limits the theatre to those symbols that provoke the most immediate understanding and response; symbols that will expose both the complexity and significance of dramatic story, characters, and crisis simultaneously. To accomplish all this, a certain bluntness is necessary. In recent years the result has been a catalog of symbols including bananas, goats, beatniks, emotionally castrated men, neurasthenic women, urinals and subway cars, imaginary children, beds, boils, and bugs, Ping-Pong balls and nerve pills and knives, poisoned dogs and dying grandmothers—the list could go on, developing, like assembled mosaic chips, a pretty terrifying picture itself.

But a symbol derives its force from the concentrated energies and understandings of the context from which they are drawn. And if the context—the climate of contemporary life—is handicapped in the kind of energies it can supply, the theatre is handicapped also.

Clearly, throughout all these remarks, there is a strong, unspoken implication that I will attempt to spell out: a society gets the kind of theatre it deserves. If the society is troubled, inferior, or unresolved as to its ultimate commitments and its postures of faith toward itself, the theatre will mirror the trouble, the inferiority, and the lack of resolution with a vividness and clarity that is stunning. It can do nothing else because, to survive, it must carve the signs that can be most widely read. The artist may choose to use the signs to comment on the state of things, to moralize a little perhaps, and even to prophesy the consequences of what he sees. He may even be bold and use the signs to change the future as Brecht tried to do. But the signs can radiate no more or no less than a public—having chosen or having imposed on them certain filters through which they are obliged to view their own lives—will see in them.

The economics of the legitimate theatre (which, for better or worse, remains a major indicator of theatrical health in the country) is now almost legendary in dimensions and popular understanding. What reasonably educated, moderately intelligent man has not heard about the meager thirty-five antiquated playhouses left on Broadway (down from seventy in 1928), the astronomical production costs (up 300–400 per cent in twenty-five years), the prohibitive ticket prices, the financial outrages committed by the profiteering middlemen, the discriminatory taxation of places and events of entertainment, the restrictive fire regulations that effectively prevent a theatre building from deriving income from anything but the putting on of plays, the constantly escalating union demands, the conniving of theatre owners to force a moderately successful play out of the theatre to make room for a more profitable product, and the exorbitant salary demands of stars fighting to stay famous in a shrinking, fiercely competitive market? Who hasn't heard all this? It is on the commercial stage, Edward Albee once observed, that you find the true theatre of the absurd. It is here that we also rediscover the bases for the "complete hit" syndrome displayed by professional producers who must live with the haunting statistic: four out of five plays will fail.

The necessity for complete, 100 per cent smash hit has some curious, corrupting side effects. Perhaps the least of them is the compulsion to puff, to inflate, and to doctor and edit reviews until, in some cases, the critic can scarcely identify what he wrote, or discovers he is suddenly ecstatic over a play that made him ill. (Things once were worse, however. The Schuberts used to buy favorable notices until Alexander Wolcott wrote an unsubsidized, unfavorable review. Supported by *The New York Times,* Wolcott's rebellion finally caused the Schuberts to back down.) Such puffing and editing results, obviously, in considerable distortion of a play's significance and impact, enticing and often betraying potential customers with quoted snippets from reviews that are themselves products of an obscure and often uninformed critical ethic.

Another and perhaps the most morbid of these side effects is the self-induced schizophrenic atmosphere that envelops a show as it nears production date. Reason and patience vanish. There is a frantic, almost compulsive attack on the script and on the staging. A 20,000 dollar garden staircase unit is suddenly singled out as culprit and thrown out of the show; the star, claiming omniscience and an aesthetic authority that was never his in the first place, declares that the second act never *did* develop the clear motivation for his behavior and wants it immediately re-rewritten. What will "work"—because it *seemed* to work for another show —is more important than what is *right*. And somewhere, closeted in a hotel room, the author sits, in a numbing whirlpool of doubt, frenzy, and frustration, having long since either forgotten or abandoned that original and radiant dream he once hoped to share with the world.

What a mockery, really, of the uncountable centuries of man's groping toward the means of a rational representation of himself; for the means of dispassionately refining his experiences into a distilled, cogent, and selective form that best expresses his most universal aspirations. It's hardly a wonder, then, that aberrant and transient dramatic forms keep appearing: the Theatre of the Absurd, of the Cruel; the naïve meanderings of the Off-Off-Broadway playlets, and the calculated chaos of the so-called "Happenings." We deserve them; we need them as a periodic spring theatre cleaning to remind us how much rubbish has collected in the legitimate theatre.

A third side effect is the obvious reluctance of a producer to be brave in the face of such a sudden death situation. If the lack of bravery were merely an uncomplicated statement of cowardice it could be understood and respected. Timidity, however, seems to have become a ruling ethic, a way of life, inspiring a deeply enervating lack of faith in one's own rational processes that has a dangerously pervasive effect, so pervasive as to pierce the footlights and contaminate the audience. Such timidity inspires producers to avoid sophomoric altruisms about the health of the American theatre in favor of tested methods for ensuring a reasonable degree of success. (Note, please: Not drama, not art, not a reasonably enduring statement of either the grandeur or frailty of man, but success. The provincial theatres and the universities have moved in to pick up the pieces of drama and art and try to put them back together.)

What are these tested methods?

1. Produce a famous playwright. Fine. But Albee, Williams, Inge, and to some extent Miller—the four horsemen of the 20th-century apocalypse—have so far found 1966 a most inhospitable year.

2. Produce a musical. Also fine. Nearly half of the offerings of the last five seasons have been musicals. But the producer better have one hundred thousand dollars or more to get it into rehearsal, and be ready, as the producers of *Kelly* were, to drop it all in one night, or to be satisfied with ersatz, synthetic, imitative, and gimmicky star vehicles. The musical has always been a measure of America's creative genius—if we are prepared to confine the examples of this genius to the fingers of one hand. I don't have to name them.

3. Adapt a famous book. Also very fine. The fact that a novel and a play have virtually nothing in common except, perhaps, the use of the English language, doesn't seem to disturb too many people. Adapting from the French of Monsieur So-and-so, from the Book-of-the-Month Club thriller of Miss Whoever, from the Jamaican folk legends compiled by Mr. What's-his-name may preserve the built-in approbation of the public, the tested and sanctified nature of the original work, but it generally guarantees nothing. There have been so many adaptations in recent years that they seemed to have become the rule rather than the exception, causing the wary critic of the *Christian Science Monitor* once to ask, "Is the fact not symptomatic of commercial timidity, or of a certain aesthetic dryness? Or both?"

4. Finally, the fourth tested method is to import a foreign production. This is an especially fine device. It has "class." The literate, clean-speaking and suave British actors, the austere and highly disciplined performers of the *Comédie Française,* and the nearly legendary skills of the Moscow Art Theatre bring considerable grandeur and not a little gratuitous identification of the producer as an astute internationalist and bringer of High Culture. Fine. We need and respect these foreign companies. We have much to learn from them in the way of ensemble acting styles, diction, and their intense dedication to an ideal about the theatre. But the motive for bringing them here is often suspect. We too often detect a zesty opportunism, an effort to protect all flanks while cashing in on the ready-made reputation of the foreign company. Pointing out, at one time, what must have seemed like another British Occupational Force ensconced in one-third of the American playhouses—strikingly reminiscent of 1778—members of Actor's Equity violently protested, threatening to hold an actors' Tea Party. Placards reading "New York is a British Festival" were carried about in union meetings, with considerable wrath directed at the Immigration Department for freely issuing work permits to foreign actors, while American actors could come by them only dearly when trying to secure work in London.

The clamor has subsided somewhat because no one wishes to exclude Olivier or Morley or Guinness or Gielgud or Scofield. The fraternity of actors is too strong for that. But the rationale behind these imports remains clear enough. Prompted by the imminent threat of financial disaster, American producers have been willing to abandon American actors, thus intensifying an already depressing situation.

Ironically, the motive behind these "tested methods" is not altogether money. Money is plentiful, especially with the recording and film industries putting up most of it. In this notably affluent society, however, there can be no fixed price for Vision, no price tag that will overcome the economic terrors and the permanently shattered images, no cost accounting that will minimize the essential greed that prompts much of the activity. Marston Balch, writing in *Prologue,* the publication of the Tufts University Theatre, remarked that "a theatre which, like Broadway today, can tolerate only smash hits and which exists on sufferance of expense account and theatre-party audiences is enslaved to an endless quest for sensation or soothing amusement, for such an audience pays to escape its condition, not to face it." This is the nub—the tragic core of "Broadway economics"—and its omnipresent specter penetrates into the deepest fibers of the American creative spirit, darkening the hope of achieving *as a people* a theatre worthy of our nation's stature—"a theatre," Balch concludes, "that can induce creative genius to turn to drama as a life goal."

Indeed, theatre economics ultimately does playgoers, and the American public in general, a profound disservice. If, as history and native experience tell us, art is the celebration of man's desire to preserve his most meaningful impressions of his universe, and if we persist in believing, as we must, that the theatre is a legitimate art form, then the commercial theatre today has sold us out. It is a dependent, irresponsible, redundant theatre, falsifying reality with cunning disguises of realism, reducing ideas and ideals to mere distractions, and ultimately punishing the artistic conscience of the country by its paralyzing lack of courage. Judging by the lack of enthusiasm for new plays displayed on many university campuses, we may rightly suspect that this paralysis is of the creeping variety.

And yet, it's hard to blame the theatre for its current behavior. If any of us were raised in the atmosphere of distrust, suspicion, and moral outrage that the American theatre suffered, we would behave strangely too. Out of the three hundred and forty years of American theatre history, one curious and continuing dilemma emerges: the United States never seemed to associate a developing civilization with a living theatre. In fact, one of the more regular gestures of American civic life—at least as represented by whatever Establishment was in force—was to actively dismiss, suppress, and outlaw the theatre, as if it were some undesirable and haphazard weed growing in an otherwise tidy garden.

Indeed, the history of the American attitude toward the theatre—and not, please note, toward "entertainment"— would, if sung, sound like a dirge. There are reasons enough to explain this attitude. In England by 1620, the Elizabethan grandeur had been harvested and stored away to dry out. The endowments of Shakespeare, Marlowe, Greene, Lyly, and Kyd were now something of an embarrassment to the more austere sovereigns and to the sensibilities of Mr. Cromwell. The quarter-century of political expansiveness and artistic vigor that marked the reign of Elizabeth I withered into sanctimonious piety, with its attendant hypersensitivity to matters of the flesh, to the extent that what theatre was tolerated became maudlin, sentimental, domestic, and finally forgotten. This was the society, we may recall, that was ashamed of Shakespeare because he was so brutal, so barbaric, and so honest. Out of this milieu of artistic mortification came the "founding fathers" of America.

All this suggests that the Pilgrims chose, from the standpoint of theatre history, the worst possible time to emigrate. Fifty years one way or the other might have made some difference; but fate, religious controversy, and the mercenary interests of certain land and trading companies willed it otherwise.

Having emigrated, the early settlers encountered a forbidding and unexplored geography, a dominion with a harsh climate and a harsh God. They found enemies skulking in the forests and other enemies, perfumed if unpainted, skulking in Parliament. And with cultural roots still raw from sudden exposure and transplant, the settlers could only view the theatre as a piece of pure frivolity.

With Cotton Mather vigorously identifying witches and warlocks that only flame, rope, and heavy stone could subdue, and with Jonathan Edwards somewhat later threatening his followers with roaring hellfires to purify their sinful souls, the theatre got off to a fitful start.

Out of this gloomy context emerged two specific notions that were to have immediate and profound effects on the theatre. The first was that any form of amusement—which might include birdstuffing, hairdressing, and playacting—had to be condemned, as both the Connecticut and Massachusetts legislatures did condemn by law in the early 1700's as "Painted Vanities." To ensure proper respect for the law, Connecticut provided for "thirteen stripes on the bare back" for anyone caught acting anything, anywhere. As early as 1667, in fact, a small group of college boys were haled into court in Accomac County, Virginia, for performing an innocuous little piece entitled "Ye Cub and Ye Bear." (We haven't changed much. Two hundred and thirty-two years later, in 1905, the Commissioner of Vice for New York City dragged the whole Arnold Daly company into court for degrading the good society of the city by performing Bernard Shaw's *Mrs. Warren's Profession*.)

The second notion involved the new land itself. Whatever its character, its promise or its native inhabitants, the land had to conform to the prepackaged laws and codes of invaders. Not an unjust practice, really, except when it is arbitrary and inflexible, thus denying the land its opportunity to shape and enrich the invaders. One apparent result of this imposition of rigid attitudes and practices is that it took nearly 150 years to stabilize the Eastern seaboard and to endow it with any kind of social coherence.

But in the hands of those men and women—the so-called pioneers, frontiersmen, riverboatmen—who responded to the character of the land itself until they virtually became a part of it, it took only about fifty years to stretch the territorial possessions of the United States literally from coast to coast. From the East only the Yankee emerged as a native Amercan type; from the West an abundance of real and legendary figures appeared: Johnny Appleseed, Paul Bunyan, Mike Fink, and Dan'l Boone.

Both the scorn of theatrical entertainments by a struggling agrarian and resolutely pious society and the ardent preservation of old country ideals and attitudes by a transplanted society are entirely reasonable patterns of human behavior. It was the prolonged rigidity of these patterns, however, that was most responsible for the stifling of many of the natural and cultural resources of the land itself. We are still paying dearly for this restraint, as evidenced by the so-called "cultural gap" that continues to exist between what we have and what we can do with it, by the regular migration of artists for foreign parts (led, long ago, by the painter John Singleton Copley and the actor-playwright John Howard Payne), by the uneasy overtures of the federal government to dabble in the arts, and by the recent Lincoln Theatre season in which American plays are embarrassingly missing.

There are many specific manifestations of the two notions the settlers brought with them. The history of the American theatre is studded with many more examples of attacks on our friend Tinker Bell than on moments of signal achievement in which the drama became a pliant and expressive instrument of the monumental struggle of the American character to reveal itself. A few of these examples, chosen at random:

1. In the face of war, among the first decisions of the Continental Congress was to declare the theatre illegal, and

drive the one decent company of players (the Hallams) out of the country to Jamaica.

2. For nearly seventy-five years following the Revolutionary War, the theatre had to be disguised as a "Moral Lecture" in order to appease the pious. By moving underground, the atmosphere of hypocrisy was intensified, making it all the harder to shake.

3. As traveling companies risked the hazards of a barge trip up the Erie Canal or penetrated the Cumberland Gap, they encountered town fathers who would levy a heavy tax on the players for the right to perform—a fee often in excess of what the players could expect to receive at the box office.

4. The great stars of the American stage throughout the 19th century made a practice of mercilessly bleeding theatre-owners by exorbitant percentage demands—with the unhappy result of forcing the closure of the very theatre the stars needed to play in.

5. The major playhouses themselves—the notorious Park and the infamous Bowery Theatre in New York City —were great, dank, barnlike structures, featuring boxes and stalls that appeared, to one contemporary observer, "like pens for animals." The gallery gods of the third tier caroused, fought, drank, and bombarded the audience in the pit, Washington Irving reported, with apple cores and other debris. Candles sputtered, and oil lamps cast a dense pall of smoke over the stage; gas jets smelled, flared, and often exploded. Vituperative exchanges between leading men and disgruntled spectators in the first balcony frequently interrupted the performance. Prostitutes solicited, policemen patrolled, actors bellowed, and, as a British visitor recorded in her diary, on one occasion a mother was seen performing "the most maternal office" for her infant. There were exceptions to these conditions, but they were rare. Having loudly foresworn—as a point of national

honor—the culturally elite and socially stratified attitude of its European counterpart, the American audience was aggressively partisan, boisterous, and ultrademocratic. The American playhouse, despite the effort to install some of the architectural delicacies that were the rage in 18th- and 19th-century British theatres, remained, essentially, the social hall, the meeting house, the forum for the expression of fiercely egalitarian notions. This was the theatre we inherited from the 19th century.

6. Not much improvement could be noted as the 20th century began. Performers generally—but specialty performers (vaudeville and later burlesque entertainers) in particular—were subjected to the grossest physical discomfort at work and the most barbaric treatment away from the theatre. It was not uncommon to find entertainers forced to use the back alleys to change, dress, or relieve themselves, or to be dispatched to grimy corners of the theatre cellar to find dressing-room facilities; or to have theatre-managers behave in a whimsical and arbitrary fashion when the payroll was due, often reneging on contracts because the "house was poor" on a particular evening or the actor was five minutes late for a call. To be sure, many actors deserved these indignities; but the managers, it seems, were retaliating with perhaps more zeal than necessary for the indignities heaped on them a century earlier.

7. The 20th century has had its own special way of demoralizing the theatre through a series of irrational confusions, or substitutions, in which Art has been made to bear the burden, or the blame, for the transient preoccupations and fancies of a given era.

As the century turned, so did the businessman—into the dominant figure in the American theatre. What had been a dominating ethic for two centuries now became, in the hands of the notorious "Theatrical Syndicate," a highly organized, immeasurably profitable, and deeply cynical

business trust that quite literally ruled nearly half the playhouses in the country. The confusion of Art with Com-
merce was irrevocably sealed in a way that was uniquely
American. Under the authoritarian rule of Messrs. Klaw,
Erlanger, Zimmerman, Nixon, and Hayman, the theatre
had finally reached the same degree of organization, mass
production, and business efficiency that the Industrial Revolution had been bringing to the economy of the entire country in the previous century. To play in a Syndicate house
meant that you hereinafter played *only* in other Syndicate-
controlled houses. To defy such an agreement meant professional death. A non-Syndicate house might appeal for
a Syndicate-controlled star or show, but it would have to
take the whole package, under Syndicate regulations and
percentages, or get nothing. The Syndicate was, of course,
broken in the early 20th century by a combine that was not
noticeably more altruistic in their designs: the brothers Sam,
Lee, and J. J. Schubert.

Art was confused with politics in the late 1930's when
the celebrated Federal Theatre, after five years of attempting to regenerate the natural, artistic resources of the country by putting unemployed actors, dancers, singers, and
musicians back to work, met a dismal death at the hands
of a senatorial investigating committee. When Hallie Flanagan, the national director of the Federal Theatre, was
brought before the committee, dark innuendos of Communist influence were alluded to, with especial reference to
Miss Flanagan's remark about certain theatres having a
"Marlowesque madness." "You are quoting from this Marlowe," observed a legislator. "Is he a Communist?" Knowing that eight thousand persons might lose their jobs
because of a bureaucratic boob, Miss Flanagan answered
crisply: "Put in the record that he was the greatest dramatist
in the period of Shakespeare, immediately preceding
Shakespeare." The final blow came shortly after the Federal

Theatre was voted out of existence. Miss Flanagan received a phone call from another congressman who wanted to talk about the theatre project in his state. When she informed him of recent congressional action of this matter—that the Federal Theatre was abolished—she heard a shocked and heavy voice in the receiver: "Was *that* the Federal Theatre?"

There are still too many who remember, or who can imagine such an exchange, and who are understandably reluctant to believe that the federal government can ever offer more than appropriately flowing words, a bundle of cash, and a profound misunderstanding of the role and the imperatives of art of a national scale.

Art has been confused with personal conscience in the case of Arthur Miller, who was refused a passport he had requested in order to attend a production of *The Crucible* in Belgium. There was no basis for the refusal, except that the House Committee on Un-American Activities exerted pressure on the State Department as a waspish and punitive measure against Miller for refusing to divulge names of friends who might have had Communist leanings. Somewhat later, Joseph Papp was also called before the same committee to be questioned about the possibility that he was slipping left-wing propaganda into his free Shakespeare productions of *Troilus and Cressida* and *Coriolanus*.

Finally, art has been—and continues to be—confused with public morality. Ironically, this has been occurring, unexpectedly, in educational institutions: those establishments dedicated, ostensibly, to acts of maximum inquiry into and confrontation with those truths—pleasant or not —that describe the human condition. So long as it is one school's or one church's view of the nature of this condition there is no problem. The officials at Baylor University forced the closing of a production of *Long Day's Journey into Night* on the grounds that the play presented an unwholesome view of life. (The staff of the Baylor Drama

Department promptly resigned.) A drama professor at Middle Tennessee University chose the opening night of a student production of *Dylan* to be seized by a bad case of scruples and public interest and stood at the theatre entrance to turn away the audience—saving them, apparently, from the dirty words spoken by the actors.

These examples are neither the only nor the most outrageous affronts to the spirit of Tinker Bell. Nor are they the only indications of the continuing erosion of theatre as a living embodiment of certain transcendent truths about birth, life, and death. They do represent, however the paltriness of spirit, the vacuity of thought, and the encrusted opportunism that seem to be the hallmarks of the contemporary theatre in both its economic and historical postures. In all fairness, it must be noted that these hallmarks are not the exclusive property of the legitimate, commercial New York stage. They occur in an infinite number of settings, wherever pretension is greater than ability, wherever enthusiasm is mistaken for vision, wherever skill is substituted for talent, and wherever the noble and elusive art of dramaturgy is reduced to an unwilling vehicle for temporary titillations or vacant prophesying.

That these hallmarks exist in the contemporary theatre is, I'm afraid, true enough. That they have always existed is also true. (I have no evidence to support it, but I'm quite certain that an ancient Greek choregus—what we would call a producer—must have been accused of seeding a Sophoclean chorus with intimate friends or of backing a Euripedes trilogy less to glorify the gods than to solidify his own status among the literati of Athens.) A continuity of evil, however, neither justifies nor softens what we are obliged to live with now. That these hallmarks continue to exist, to soak into the roots of American culture, and continue to produce deformed shapes that mock and scandalize any notion of a progressive civilization is bad enough. To acknowledge, as we must, that many of these hallmarks are self-consciously employed and cynically accepted by producers, writers, directors, actors, critics, and teachers is the real source of melancholy.

We have briefly examined three of the possible causes of death: the nature of theatre art itself, the economic implications of the professional stage, and the historical infringements on a free and flourishing drama. There is one more area to consider.

We know that every reasonably defined age—whether Bronze, Enlightenment, or Nuclear—transmits a distinctive character of its own. The character of an age, like that of a man, is usually a composite of dominant traits and attitudes that express the special longings and terrors of the era. I can't pretend to have identified all the traits and attitudes that constitute the 20th-century character or even to understand fully those that have been identified for me by social and cultural historians. But insofar as the theatre is concerned, it is possible to isolate those strong currents in contemporary thought and behavior that express our own unique vision—or lack of one—of the universe. And if this vision is contradictory, ambiguous, searching, or unsatisfying, then the theatre, obliged to mirror and reckon with the real imperatives of the society which sustains it, must reflect thought and behavior that is contradictory, ambiguous, searching, and unsatisfying.

Only two seemingly characteristic attitudes are worth mentioning here because of their especially telling effect on the theatre. First, a fearful imbalance continues to exist between the nature of life and the function of art. It is so out of proportion, in fact, that there is almost an inbred lack of faith in the efficacy of art (in general) and the theatre (in particular) to fulfill its primary duty: to cause the infinitely random impressions of man and nature to coalesce into a meaningful, necessary, and superior revela-

tion of life's purpose. This weakness of faith in the traditional function of the artist has been, indeed, one of the
noticeably tragic flaws in the American character; not,
mind you, in the *appreciation* of an artist's skills in content
and style. We are uncommonly adept at labeling, identifying, categorizing, and tossing off succulent phrases about
Gaugin's "primitivism" or the "emotional deformities" in
Tennessee Williams or Henry Moore's "negative space."
We are great consumers of product and product informa-
tion. But art as a natural and native experience, rivaling
the intimate and immediate satisfactions of, say, the dreams
we all share of success in health, wealth, and love, or of
profound religious experience, is alien to most Americans.
This is not intended as a bitter denunciation of us boorish
Americans. Rather, it is a way of saying that we have not
found an enduring means of accommodating the satisfactions peculiar to art—in any of its manifestations—to the
velocity and intensity of a burgeoning, pragmatic culture.
In short, we are too busy absorbing the mammoth complexities and anxieties of living to have time to develop the
qualities of critical reflection and personal taste (based on
knowledge and experience rather than on mere intuition)
so basic to the indivisibility of art and life.

As it happens, art continues to be very much divisible
from the common fund of the American experience. It
seems, at times, to be gratuitous, extraneous, something of
an afterthought (the way communities across the country
are furiously afterthinking and hastily erecting Cultural
Centers as their way of belatedly propitiating the impatient
Muses and other well-endowed civic leaders), indeed,
rather as an embellishment to man's otherwise banal and
mechanical existence. And so long as art remains divisible,
the theatre will be embarrassed by it (as will be discovered
in a subsequent chapter on the lamentable story of poets
in the theatre), and will strive to conceal it by taking refuge

in the short-range dodge of providing "entertainment." Art and life exist, ideally, in a strange and fragile kind of equipoise, each constantly trying to outstrip the other, each trying to stay abreast of and to contain one another. The painter, the sculptor, the composer may take upward leaps in their experiments with materials, tonalities, and styles; and life must rush to catch up, to realize it has been missing out on certain abstract concepts of the world.

But the theatre cannot risk such experiments, being confined to representations of mortal experience and mortal flesh in their most widely understood forms. It tries to stay in perfect balance with life. And when, either through periods of creative drought or through periods of national or global crises so vast that the human imagination is numbed, the delicate balance shifts abruptly, the theatre can no longer contain it. It seems paltry by comparison, lagging behind and enfeebled. Indeed, of the various "traits" of the American national character today, it is this pronounced and aggravated gulf that exists between the nature of life and the function of art in the theatre that is the most awesome.

Perhaps the theatre, as we know it, is defunct and simply doesn't have the wisdom to lay down. With motion pictures and television having outstripped the theatre in their ability to reproduce credible and comprehensive views of life, the theatre may have to search for a new form, to stop trying to give artificial life to a dead realism. It's interesting, of course, to note that as a result of this gulf writers and producers have been desperately trying to compensate by offering up massive dollops of (1) nostalgia (*Hello, Dolly!* and *Fiddler on the Roof*), (2) sensual violence and cruelty (*The Devils* and *Marat/Sade*), or (3) homosexuality (any number of plays).

The second trait is one which professional theologians or social scientists could probably deal with much better.

It's the problem of what might be called a moral relativism —or, "How do I know what's right any more?" The moral and ethical signposts that once designated paths of Wisdom, Truth, Virtue, Religiosity, that once promised material security, political flexibility, and social harmony, seem now to be only dimly identified or barely remembered. The ethical incongruities we once—in our childhood, I suppose, if then—thought impossible, have become realities of the human condition. I'm making no moral judgment, sighing over lost Boy Scout verities or that "old time Religion." Maybe there never was much practicality about either to begin with. Nor am I getting sober-sided or blue-stockinged about the prevalence of "smut," lurid sex crimes or the incidence of narcotics among teen-agers of upper income families. Everyone's got his problems.

I'm talking about those bolder, darker lines of moral attitude that are born of a fixed conviction that there is, somewhere, justice; that there must be, somewhere, a boundary line dividing honor from dishonor; that there has to be, somehow, one enormous Truth to counterbalance the infinity of little lies we tell ourselves and that we are fed regularly by the professional cynics that infest every major institution and enterprise. Do the bold, darker lines exist at all? Certainly they do; they are hard to find, however.

And the consequences to the theatre are enormous. The concept of the hero, for instance, has suffered most. Once, we could identify the hero, suffer with him, celebrate him in our hearts; we could die with him, if necessary, because in his death we might be reborn a little. Even the villain was a joy to identify and have around, not because it was *simple* to point to the good guy and the bad guy, but because we could take the measure of good and evil in accordance with whatever standard of conduct and behavior we believed in ourselves. If such a standard is no longer practicable, the impact of virtually all human action is drastically reduced, making any hero-concept (as we will see in a later chapter) seem to be a peculiar 20th-century anachronism.

If we now believe in no standard of behavior, or if, in response to the proverbial complexity of 20th-century life, we are willing to adjust, to modify, and to compromise what seems to be, after all, pretty tenuous and naïve beliefs, how may we judge the stature and significance of a dramatic character—who itself is a symbol of moral pliancy and ethical drift? But above all, how shall we judge ourselves? If both Right and Wrong are fogged in, where do we land? Is there an alternate field?

These are, clearly, rhetorical questions, certainly unanswerable by me and, to some extent, even by skilled theologians and social historians who are still struggling to redefine the nature of personal conscience and morality in a universe that has been cunningly conspiring to thwart both for centuries. But, again, such questions plague the theatre, which is obliged to confirm the case of moral relativism. It is right for the theatre to do this. We can only wish that a distant drummer were louder. Or that there were a distant drummer.

Well, this has been a lengthy autopsy on Tinker Bell. Results: death by vulnerability, by economic pressure on the aesthetic mechanism, by historical oppression, and by a general weakness in the upper morality.

Tinker Bell is gone. Or was she ever around? Her absence has had one unsurprising effect: redeemers, diagnosticians, and prognostics have rushed—belatedly—to the graveside with proposals for saving the theatre, for pumping fresh blood into its shrunken carcass; to apologize for and theorize about the awful state of the drama.

Out of the abundance of prescriptions and controversies have come four sure-fire remedies: awaken the Tragic Muse, stimulate the hearts of Poets, locate the source of

Heroes, and identify the Moral Blight that covers the land —and thus the theatre. The next four chapters will examine the remedies individually, starting with Eugene O'Neill's fitful efforts to define the shape of a tragic grandeur appropriate to the American experience and beneficial to the American theatre.

ii

O'Neill and the Passing of Pleasure

The American theatre has not yet recovered from its collision with Eugene O'Neill. Although the bulk of his major writings are today more often politely patronized than actively produced, O'Neill's real impact on the 20th-century theatre resulted from the way he threatened it: he demanded that it be bigger, better, and more prophetic than it was. To substantiate his threat, O'Neill appointed himself chief Visionary-Laureate of the American drama.

Perhaps he knew what he was getting himself into. Certainly O'Neill saw his task in passionately simple terms: to find an epic means of expressing man's patently absurd and alien role in the universe.

The job became complicated almost at once. There was, first, the vapidly sentimental and entrenched 19th-century drama that both offended and seduced O'Neill. Titanic conflicts were to ensue as O'Neill struggled to resist the facile and spurious emotional reasoning of his dramatic predecessors by using weapons—Freudian, Grecian, and nihilistic—that he could not handle comfortably.

The job became even more complicated when O'Neill, having elbowed his way onto Olympus for a better view of the frail mortals below, succumbed to the fearful realization that he was not seeing all men but a personal reflection, not a vision but a nightmare.

The American theatre, ennobled by O'Neill's cosmic pretensions and grandiose speculations, was momentarily transfixed by this nightmare; no previous playwright had so relentlessly probed into the psychic quagmires of human behavior while so thoroughly exposing himself. In retrospect, however, it's relatively easy to determine what made his role of Visionary-Laureate so unsatisfactory and his contribution to the death of Tinker Bell so substantial.

To begin with, O'Neill was a paradigm of dramaturgical incongruities. He was, for instance, a writer capable of enormous and stunning visions, but he was endowed with frail and limited equipment to capture and preserve those visions. He created an incredible gallery of human portraits and superhuman crises that were often supported by a clumsily reasoned, highly derivative philosophy—Nietzschean, mostly, and Freudian, too. O'Neill was a godless, despondent, pessimistic, antisocial creature who was also prone to such exuberance that he could write to a friend, "I'm tickled to death with life! I wouldn't 'go out' and miss the rest of the play for anything!" He was a functioning artist who regularly betrayed the artist's function by being unable to separate, to "distance," himself enough from his material to exert a few of the artist's basic obligations: compression, economy, clarity.

He was, finally, a writer so plagued by the inadequacy of the medium in which he was writing and so tortured by the abundance of his feelings that he picked, used, and discarded theatrical forms and styles with an ease that bordered on frivolity. The results: he perfected no form, enriched no style, endowed the theatre with nothing more than the terrifying spectacle of a man who could find neither meaning in life nor purpose in death. A considerable endowment to be sure; but it's unsettling to find that the theatre has matured as the result of a man's nightmare rather than his artistry.

Shakespeare welded the chronicle history, the medieval morality, and the lyrical poem into a distinctive dramatic form. Molière fused the buffoonery of the Italian slapstick comedy—the commedia dell'arte—with the elegance of the court dance and created a vivid genre of satire. Sophocles, to go all the way back, stirred together religious mysteries, popular myths, and poetry to produce the celebrated Attic tragedy of Ancient Greece. O'Neill, like a housewife in the supermarket, picked one of everything on the shelf: realism, naturalism, expressionism, Freudian analysis, historical drama. This is not to minimize O'Neill's efforts or intentions. He was compulsive, even desperate to find some container, *any* container powerful and pliant enough to hold his vision.

That he made these random selections explains, in part, the skepticism of many modern critics. To try anything is fine; it's a necessary part of flexing one's aesthetic muscles, of growing up. To have resolved nothing, to have synthesized nothing is not so fine. To stir up artistic embers without rekindling a flame is merely to remind us that the embers are close to extinction.

Yet they glowed intensely—for thirty-seven years and through forty-five plays. Ironically, only near the end, with the completion of *Long Day's Journey into Night,* after titanic encounters with demons and emotional eruptions that shook his own foundations—if not the theatre's—did the embers finally ignite. And only because a measure of peace if not, indeed, exhaustion, had made it possible to come to terms with the haunting specter of an unfulfilled image of himself.

Great writers are marked, as a rule, by fierce preoccupations, by nagging perplexities and tensions that constitute a kind of perpetual subtext to their lives. Out of this subtext comes what we call the writer's *vision,* the special stance he takes that helps him see the world steadily and see it whole, as Thomas Hardy put it. For most writers, the vision can be fairly objectified, fairly well reasoned, as if they were watching the world from the roof of a tall building, unnoticed, privy to the unconscious actions and thoughts of the men below them.

Since the Second World War, the preoccupations of the major playwrights have been fairly evident: life is so absurd and so oppressive that man has been eroded, his pretensions shriveled into mocking echoes of himself, his identity in doubt, his value in question. He is unable, like Willy Loman, to separate true from false myth—if there was ever a separation; unable, like Branche DuBois, to recognize the decay in his soul; unable, like George and Martha, to acknowledge that Albee's miserable couple are feeding the inferno that is devouring them. In the 1930's it was just as easy to isolate the dominant vision: hunger, social injustice, corrupt capitalism, a dream of a new world that would provide Joe and Edna's kids—in *Waiting for Lefty*—with the grapefruit they've never seen.

But in the past thirty-five years, none of the major professional playwrights seriously challenged the *theatre itself* as perhaps one major source of human decay. None seriously challenged *life itself*—as opposed to the transient perils and disasters of living it—as a source of human corruption. None seriously believed that tragedy—that ultimate absurdity in which man pretends he is equal to the primeval calamities of the universe—had any real meaning for anyone.

O'Neill did. And that's why he stands out both as a heroic statue, deserving of all the laurels the Nobel and Pulitzer committees heaped on him, and also as a sore thumb. To speak great prophecies to a deaf, complacent, affluent age, or to threaten that age with grave portents of man's terrible insularity is very bold and very necessary. But if you are not fully equipped to break through the deafness and complacency, or if you are still as involved in fighting a private battle as well as a universal one, there is the possibility of sounding a little silly.

If O'Neill had not been plagued by artistic handicaps that could scarcely support his towering artistic pretensions, he might have been more successful in subduing his greatest enemy—the spiritually bankrupt drama of the 19th-century American theatre. As matters turned out, he lost the battle to cleanse the theatre, to drive out those who, in O'Neill's words, "scribble on the surface of things." He lost because he was obliged to adopt the enemy's melodramatic weapons and tactics in a manner unbecoming a Visionary-Laureate of the 20th century.

It was not surprising that he lost. The drama he was fighting took itself very seriously, was immensely popular, and made a lot of money. This was the theatre of William Vaughan Moody, James A. Herne, Clyde Fitch, Edward Sheldon, and David Belasco. These were cunning dramatists, secure in their craft, deeply conscious of their moral responsibility to offer the public sober and tantalizing "truths" about mankind. Passionate loyalties, infidelities, political corruption, deathless utterances at moments of shattering revelations, the flower of love growing from the earth of lust, the valiant act performed in the teeth of death, the superhuman gesture of forgiveness, humility discovered in adversity—sounds a little like the three-hankie silent movies, oozing pathos, passion, and fraudulence. These were the themes, ingredients, and attitudes of the theatre O'Neill was nursed on and never fully escaped from.

Taken in bulk—as bulk was its chief asset—the serious theatre of, say, the fifty years before O'Neill nervously handed his first manuscript to the college kids down in Provincetown on Cape Cod in 1917 was indistinctive, transitory, melodramatic, and deeply loved. Its crimes against life were many, not the least of which was that it resolutely ignored reality. It was guilty of substituting realism for reality; of reproducing accurately the excitement of external behavior, of the clatter and crisis of surface events on the assumption that that was what was most true about life. And whenever Moody, Herne, or Fitch got into trouble—that is, when they stumbled onto a dangerously probing look at human beings—they could invoke any one of a number of patent formulas to withdraw safely: the heroine could die; the long-concealed document could be discovered; the opportunistic, ruthless social climber would—abruptly—realize he really loved the rich girl for herself alone. (Sound familiar? If the films and TV plays that had used these plots were placed end to end . . . .)

To avoid embarrassing confrontations with reality, to disguise it perhaps, or perhaps even in utter innocence of life, the theatre prior to O'Neill was a theatre of "great moments"; sensational and stunning events were calculated to awe and to transfix an audience where they sat. These could take the form of mechanical wonders, such as in the amazing "dark-to-dawn" sequence in Belasco's *Madame Butterfly*. (The stage direction reads: "During the vigil, the night comes on. Suzuki lights the floor lamps, the stars come out, the dawn breaks, the floor lights flicker out one by one, the birds begin to sing, and the day discovers Suzuki and the baby fast asleep on the floor." Think of the magic involved; the shades of purple, red, orange, yellow; the stars piercing the black heavens; the sound effects. Imagine the gasping as the audience was held enthralled for fifteen to twenty minutes while the spectacle was unfolded.) The "great moment" could be the act of hair-raising bravery, as when Davy Crockett, using the strong right arm of the woodsman, bars the door against the attacking wolves. Or the unbearable suspense in William Vaughan Moody's *The Great Divide* when the heroine engages the sheriff in a card game to protect her wounded lover, who is hiding directly above them in the attic. The game is played slowly and deliberately. The sheriff is almost convinced by the heroine's nonchalance when a single drop of blood falls from above onto the back of the sheriff's hand. A great moment, indeed.

I'm ignoring, of course, the so-called popular theatre, the prevaudeville stage, that enjoyed its own brand on inanities: cheap melodramas especially rigged so that heroes could be snatched from the jaws of giant cranes or cross to safety, carrying a lighted dynamite bomb, on a telegraph wire; so that trained dogs, horses, or bears could plunge into burning buildings to save the assorted babies that were invariably left lying about; so that ex-prizefighters and ex-safecrackers could demonstrate their specialties; so that Indian chiefs, geisha girls, and wall-scaling Zoave troops from North Africa could parade about, somewhat pointlessly, to decorate the proceedings.

Of the various forms of drama that are ancestral to O'Neill, perhaps a good example is James A. Herne's domestic melodrama *Margaret Fleming*. Let me relate the plot—without comment: Philip Fleming, a well-to-do mill owner, is told that his former mistress has just given birth to his son. Philip's first thoughts are to keep this from his wife, Margaret, who has just given birth to his daughter. Philip is told by Dr. Larkin that Lena Schmidt, the mistress, is dying and that he (Philip) had better do his duty by her. In the meantime, Dr. Larkin discovers that Margaret has an eye disorder that could leave her blind if she receives any great shocks. As fate will have it, Maria Bindley, the nurse to the Fleming baby, is also the sister of Lena Schmidt and has sworn to kill the man who has done her sister ill. Maria asks Margaret if she would please go to see her dying sister. Margaret does go, but before she gets there Lena dies, leaving a note naming the father of her child. On Margaret's arrival, Maria starts shouting and cursing at her, claiming Philip to be the father. Shocked by this, Margaret does go blind. Philip leaves home feeling very ashamed, and Margaret takes the baby boy home with her. After a week's time, Philip returns asking for forgiveness and love from Margaret. Margaret, being noble, states that only time will bring back love.

It must have been hard for anyone with so restless and thirsty a spirit as O'Neill's to look out over the drought-stricken theatre of the *Margaret Fleming* ilk and to wonder if it was salvageable at all. The prospect must have distressed him profoundly, because it surely seemed to be but another dark fragment in a never-ending series of contradictions, lies, and incompatibilities that had been undermining the American drama for years. The stage, O'Neill felt, *could* be an instrument of truth. It had to be for him; no other literary medium appealed to him once he got past the stage of adolescent verse. Not only an instrument, but a *personal* instrument; and if the instrument was defiled, so was he. And so were the multitude of anxieties and guilts that stirred within him, struggling for escape into the serenity of an artistic form. It's no wonder O'Neill "shopped around," sampling religious mysticism, expressionism, naturalism, classicism, and primitivism as possible escape routes. That his shopping ultimately failed to turn up what he was looking for was only partly the fault of the theatre; it lay less in the art than in himself.

O'Neill failed his first assignment as theatre Visionary-Laureate—that of exorcising the shabby demons that were tempting and destroying the drama. It was too big a job for any one man, especially one so obviously attracted to a style of psychological realism that had already been popularized as the "new realistic drama" of Clyde Fitch, Edward Sheldon, and James A. Herne. To beat the demons —and still find a receptive American public—O'Neill had to join them. *Beyond the Horizon, Ile, Rope, Where the Cross Is Made, Desire Under the Elms, The Great God*

Brown, Strange Interlude, and other major works, are only —in structure, language, and emotional largesse—a whisper away from *Margaret Fleming.*

But O'Neill wanted to shout, not whisper. He could accomplish this, he felt, and notably alter the character of the theatre, by fulfilling his second assignment: to infuse American drama with a jolt of epic grandeur it would not soon forget. He would have succeeded had he not confused bulk with grandeur, philosophic attitudinizing with genuine prophecy, and compulsive sufferers with Nietzschean supermen. The American theatre was already surfeited with bulk, attitudinizing, and suffering.

We have reason to suspect, as critic Robert Brustein and others have suspected, that O'Neill was self-consciously playing Literary Giant. He was afflicted, Brustein suggested, with the American disease of gigantism. To prove, perhaps, that he and his native theatre were capable of rivaling the literary output and complexity of style of anyone, O'Neill took on all comers. One of his grand conceptions—an eleven-play cycle—was to equal, he modestly suggested, *War and Peace.* The more ambitious and Olympian the competitors—and he presumed to climb into the ring with such heavyweights as Sophocles and Strindberg —the better. The growing density, ambiguity, length, and philosophic posturing of the main body of his plays testifies to the literary chest-thumping of which O'Neill was guilty, but which prompted him to indulge in the role of the dark wanderer, invested in universal visions, ready to tilt with the gods, faintly messianic, washed up on the sand dunes of Cape Cod, ready to deliver unto the world, if not the answers, at least the proper questions. God? Destiny? Immortality? Fate? Tragedy? Anyone willing—and, hopefully, able—to juggle such questions could not be all bad.

Three roads to grandeur—largely untraveled by his immediate predecessors or peers—were open to O'Neill: the pursuit of God, the return to the Greeks, and the trackless pathways of the sea.

The first road—to God—proved to be more unmarked and devious than even O'Neill suspected. To him, it was God—or at least man's relationship with a viable deity—that lay at the center of modern man's dilemma. Whether it did or not was immaterial; O'Neill felt it *ought* to be at the center of both life and the theatre. He had, we know, some keen reasons for feeling this way. The strong New England Irish Catholic tradition he was reared in—and reared, by any conventional standard, in a most disruptive and unsatisfying manner—made an especially deep imprint upon him. There was just enough instability, suspicion, and sense of bitter failure in his family life to convert an incipient rebel into a full-scale one. He was, therefore, vulnerable to the attractions of those philosophies that seemed to erase any erstwhile pretensions of man about God. It was an easy and natural step, then, from the Father, the Son, and the Holy Ghost to *Thus Spake Zarasthustra* and *The Birth of Tragedy* by Nietzsche. Both works, first encountered during his late teens, provided him with a heady rationale for rejecting the God of his fathers. The impact of these works was to be long lasting. Much later, O'Neill was to reiterate the theme of a dead God in a note to George Jean Nathan: "The playwright today must dig at the roots of the sickness of today as he feels it—the death of the Old God and the failure of science and materialism to give any satisfying new one for the surviving primitive religious instinct to find a meaning of life in, and to comfort his fears of death with."

Ultimately, O'Neill was never able to fully reject "family" with its deeply imbedded cultural traits and myths —even the one about God; and he could never fully accept the Nietzschean view that only the faithless man is truly free. Caught between a primitive myth and a contemporary fact, O'Neill could not, finally, construct an epic grandeur for the American theatre out of any tenable God-image. That the image was a blank was hardly a very comforting thought, but it signalized an influential quantum jump in the intellectual arsenal of contemporary playwrights.

The second road—back to the Greeks—didn't contribute noticeably to the restoration of grandeur either. O'Neill thought he could find security in the trappings of Greek classical myth, or at least to borrow enough of it to paste onto a new setting. The epic confrontations of the Greek tragic heroes, the sense of fate that saturated all their actions, the austerity of the dramatic form proved irresistible to O'Neill, as it has to other playwrights, namely Cocteau and Giradoux. It seemed perfect: the Greek tragic hero was a man driven toward and obsessed by the inevitability of his own doom, just as O'Neill himself, and his characters after, were driven and obsessed. And what probably appealed to O'Neill most was the promise of catharsis—the cleansing of the soul through pity and terror. So fascinated was O'Neill by the prospects of restructuring Greek drama to fit contemporary needs that he spent five years painstakingly plotting out what must have seemed to him to be cunning parallels between ancient and modern figures. Between 1926 and 1931 he kept a diary on his progress with what he called his "Greek plot idea." It's an intriguing document, as much because it reveals the evolution of a particular play, *Mourning Becomes Electra,* as it clarifies—as few playwrights have attempted to clarify—the ordeal of a slowly germinating idea; a creative history, you might say.

Here are a few excerpts from the diary: "Spring—1926. Modern psychological drama using one of the old legend plots of Greek tragedy for its basic theme—the Electra story?—the Medea?" (He had already, by the way, dipped into both the Hippolytus and Medea legends for *Desire Under the Elms*. Not consciously, perhaps, but the young woman falling in love with her stepson is present, as is a mother murdering a child for revenge.) O'Neill goes on in his diary: "Is it possible to get modern psychological approximation of Greek sense of fate into such a play, which an intelligent audience of today, possessed of no belief in gods or supernatural retribution, could accept and be moved by—?" He lets the questions hang for two years. Then in October, 1928: "Greek plot idea—story of Electra and family psychologically most interesting—most comprehensive intense basic human interrelationships—can be easily widened in scope to include still other."

By April, 1929, the idea is beginning to take shape rapidly: "Lay in New England small seaport, shipbuilding town—family town's best—shipbuilders and owners—wealthy for period—Agamemnon character town's leading citizen, Mayor before war, now Brigadier General Grant's army—house Greek temple front type that was rage in 1st half 19th century—(this fits in well and absolutely justifiable, not forced Greek similarity—home of New England House of Atreus . . .)."

Now matters get tricky. He is planning a few departures that need something of a computer to sort out: "Aegithus bears strong facial resemblance to Agamemnon and Orestes—his resemblance to Orestes attracts Clytemnestra—his resemblance to her father attracts Electra—Electra adores father, devoted to brother (who resembles father), hates mother—Orestes adores mother, devoted to sister (whose face resembles mother's) so hates his father—Agamemnon, frustrated in love for Clytemnestra, adores daughter Electra, who resembles her, hates and is jealous of his son, Orestes—etc. work out this symbol of family resemblances and identification (as visible sign of the family fate) still further—use masks?"

It goes on in this vein while he tries to find euphonious equivalents for the ancient names: Orestes turns into Orin, Clytemnestra into Christine, Agamemnon becomes Mannon, and so forth. He settles on a title but then finds he has three plays going (*The Homecoming, The Hunted,* and *The Haunted*). He wrote a draft, found it was "scrawny stuff," and plunged ahead. On March 8, 1931, he reread the typescript of the third draft and announced that it "looks damned good to me."

Well, so much for the diary, for this earnest effort to hammer out a modern parable with ancient tools. The diary betrays both the loftiness of his intentions as well as their futility. Greek drama will not transport comfortably; Greek drama is not a pruned tree onto which alien branches are grafted. Greek drama was the reenactment, for essentially religious and moral purposes, of the *consequences* of fateful acts of violence or human error, not the re-creation of and reveling in the acts themselves. Greek characters were driven, truly, but by *imperfect knowledge* of the universe in which they live, not by libidinous disorders of the lower parts. To be driven by a passion is one thing; to be blinded by it is quite another. Thus, the diary is an invaluable record, but truly a rather sad one.

In contrast to God and the Greeks, O'Neill's third road to epic grandeur—the sea—seemed to offer the greatest promise as a catalyst for dramatic ideas. From the day he signed on as an ordinary seaman at Boston's Mystic Wharf to the completion of *Long Day's Journey* in 1941, the sea was a constant presence, a symbol of uncomplicated religious ecstacy and personal freedom. From the sailors in *Bound East for Cardiff* (1915) to Edmund in *Long Day's Journey* and for a total of sixteen plays in between, there is a periodic return to the sea as a means of regenerating oneself. In 1922, Paddy in *The Hairy Ape* speaks:

Oh, there was fine, beautiful ships them days—clippers with tall masts touchin' the sky. . . . Oh, to be scudding south again wid the power of the Trade Wind driving her on steady through the nights and the days! Full sail on her! . . . Nights when the foam of the wake would be flaming wid fire, when the sky'd be blazing and winking wid stars. Or the full of the moon maybe . . . Twas them days men belonged to the ships, not now. 'Twas them days a ship was part of the sea, and a man was part of a ship, and the sea joined all together and made it one.

Twenty years later, O'Neill is still at it. Edmund speaks:

I lay on the bowsprit, facing astern, with the water foaming into spume under me, the masts with every sail white in the moonlight, towering high above me. I became drunk with the beauty and singing rhythm of it, and for a moment I lost myself—actually lost my life. I was set free! . . . I belonged, without past or future, within peace and unity and a wild joy, within something greater than my own life, of the life of Man, to life itself!

But the sea was only temporary comfort. Like "Sinner Man" of the folk song, it was no place to run to for permanent solace. It could be whimsical, vicious, and turn into "dat old Devil sea." The cost of spiritual peace and emotional magnanimity ran high; the sea could be cunning and destructive, like the atavistic, primitive force that sucks the Emperor Jones back into the black night of his primeval origins or leads the Hairy Ape's steps to the city zoo and into the arms of his primate brother. O'Neill knew this, perhaps better than he knew anything else in his life. His first plays—*S.S. Glencairn, Ile, In the Zone*—reflect the potency of the sea and its effect on the character of men; how the sea can disfigure men, forcing them to regress into images of terror, madness, and despair.

So the sea didn't work out altogether too well as a catalyst to enlarge the character of the American theatre. The sea remained, instead, O'Neill's personal symbol of escape from human corruption, a device to wash away his personal identity, rather than as a means of confronting the issues of corruption and identity themselves.

Ironically, it was when O'Neill was finally driven down a road he had been avoiding all the time that he infused some real grandeur to the American theatre. The road didn't lead to God, to the Greeks, or to the sea; it led deep within the writer himself, to an exorcism of the guilt, terror, and love he felt for his dead family. It led to *Long Day's Journey into Night*. As critic John Raleigh put it: "After biblical and Greek-Civil War descents into past history, after travels in the Orient, after primitivism, after racial imbroglios (*All God's Chillun Got Wings*), after nineteenth century New England, after the sea, after Greek masks, after dynamos, after all kinds of themes and devices and bizarre subjects, he finally returned home to New London, Connecticut, to his family, and to himself."

Long Day's Journey will remain perhaps the most singular triumph of his entire career and one of the legitimate glories of the American drama. Tempered by twenty years of bravado, of ghost-hunting, of personal anguish that bordered, at times, on suicidal impulses, he was ready to face himself, somewhat more wary of the extravagances of the past. And the result was remarkable. Here is a play that derives its ultimate power *not* from plot—which is at best a crude mechanical "system"—but from a process of character revelation that is awesome in its grinding inevitability; not from the usual sordid probes into the subterranean streams of humans compulsively tearing away from one another, but from a compassionate insight into

profoundly lost humans groping blindly, sometimes vi-
ciously, often pathetically, *toward* one another; not by
melodramatic swirls and eruptions, but by a tightly compressed, well-controlled development of human interrelationships that even—as a good classical play should—observes the dramatic unities. Each character is keenly and
honestly defined as to his or her special kind of night: for
James Tyrone, it's failure through drink, incompatibility,
and raging conflicts he cannot control; for Mary, regres-
sion to childhood through drugs and a world no longer
real; for Edmund (Eugene), isolation and alienation
through tuberculosis and a prolonged Irish adolescence;
for Jaimie, death through the empty, loquacious pointlessness of his life. It's a biting tale, to be sure, but not a
morbid one. In fact, it's one of the few plays by O'Neill in
which a sense of passionate detachment is most apparent.
O'Neill, it seems, had finally nailed down an elusive truth:
the best way to play God is to know how to make Men.
We don't know that he died happier for this discovery. It
would have been too much out of character if he had. We
do know, however, that a play very much approximating
a masterwork had been created. And when the Elms, Interludes, and Electras begin to seem like quaint bits of early
Americana—as, indeed, they are beginning to seem now—
Long Day's Journey will continue to radiate an immediacy
and power that will not very likely diminish.

It has been said that the American theatre grew up as a
result of O'Neill. This is not the case. Like a zealous tailor,
he traced king-size patterns on the fabric of American
life, hoping that the garment he was making wouldn't look
too silly on the frail body of the American theatre. The
garment proved too long, too heavy, too thick; the body,
rather than filling out, got lost. To be sure, O'Neill was
more vocal than his peers, more prolific, and more susceptible to the high fashion social and psychological philos-

ophies of his day. He did, furthermore, alert the theatre to its treacherous limitations as well as its radiant possibilities. That the American drama matured with O'Neill is, for a number of reasons, an untenable notion.

O'Neill did succeed in discrediting the Theatre of Pleasure, the theatre dedicated to the brief encounter with life's little unpleasantries for the purpose of illuminating those pretty little lies about truth, beauty, and love. With the subtlety of an air hammer, O'Neill dispelled the petty fictions, the vacuous disguises, and the patent formulas that had made the theatre an escape hatch from reality.

Nearly thirty years before they became fashionable cant among intellectuals and sober playwrights, O'Neill reintroduced to the American theatre notions that threatened the placidness of society—notions of noncommunication, alienation, of purposeless drifting, and compulsive guilt; in other words, of the immutably absurd condition of man. It is in this respect that Miller, Williams, and Albee are indebted to O'Neill. He laid out, albeit crudely most of the time, the direction of American drama by isolating, albeit imprecisely as a rule, the major spiritual crises of the 20th century. As a result, writers for the American theatre could never be completely trivial or myopic again. Even the slick ones, the facile, gilt-edged writers of popular Broadway pap, have been affected, not daring to pass off mere amusement any more. Their voices may not roar like cannon over social and psychic iniquities, but they struggle to stay attuned to contemporary issues for the sake of popping off a barbed observation or two about some topical calamity. Indeed, audiences would feel cheated if there wasn't at least a garbled message coming through, in some form or other.

So O'Neill killed off Pleasure. It was ready to be killed off. It had been killing itself off for years: all O'Neill had to do was deliver the *coup de grace*. Very beneficial all around. But very sad, too, for the idea of a serious, responsible theatre is not antithetical to the idea of "entertainment." During those periods of dramatic history when the theatre was speaking in a secure voice, when form had been disciplined to accommodate the pressing subjects of the day, there was no need to make arbitrary distinctions between what was good for the soul and what was good just for the evening. O'Neill, unfortunately and perhaps inadvertently, helped soil the notion of Entertainment— which is to me (and, indeed, was to Aristotle)—a solid 50 per cent of the theatre's basic function. The verb "to entertain," free of all the usual associations of triviality, originates from the French, *"tenir"*: to hold, and *"Entre"*: between. To hold between. To hold, as it were, in suspension. In suspension between what? Between the reality of our own existence and the myth (or illusion) being perpetrated on the stage. Why? Suspend for what purpose? To make vulnerable. To sensitize an audience to a strong, and perhaps new series of impressions that their normal, sensible preoccupations might possibly blot out. Why vulnerable? Doesn't that cheapen, weaken, reduce the intelligence of an audience? No, never. The impact of a play must be, *first of all,* an *emotional* impact. It must awaken, stir, move the sense totally so that the *idea* the play is developing may be transmitted through the medium of *tension,* a medium which activates to a high degree the receptivity of an audience. Easy to achieve? Hardly. Most audiences are too reluctant, too self-contained, too intellectually superior, too suspicious of motives and techniques to turn themselves over fully to this tension. This unfortunate situation obliges playwrights who have a serious point to make, to drop the scalpel in favor of the mallet. Is this suspension a form of escapism? Entirely the reverse; it's a drawing in, not a letting out. It calls for commitment on the part of an audience, not denial. When "entertainment" is rightly and fully conceived, it frees all channels for the improved flow of serious ideas.

The most impressive and significant moments in your lives, I venture to suggest, have been *emotional* moments. I venture further to suggest that out of such moments have come whatever you believe you have "learned" about yourself, about others, about life in general. It's rarely the other way around. The theatre is no different.

O'Neill found the channels of the 19th-century theatre totally blocked by wrongly and incompletely conceived ideas about entertainment. He had to break them open. A necessary task, to be sure. But in so doing, he contributed to the killing off of Pleasure, and of our friend Tinker Bell.

A large problem connected with killing off Pleasure is to find a substitute. As we've seen, this wasn't easy for O'Neill—as it isn't for *any* playwright. But O'Neill thought he had a replacement: a vision of that "darkling plain" that Arnold describes, peopled not by "ignorant armies" but by Nietzschean supermen, superheroes, large economy size epic sufferers; by creatures capable of cataclysmic crises, with dreams bigger than the human frame can bear, with terrors and guilts deeper than the human spirit can plumb. He tried, earnestly, conscientiously, to make such embodiments of superpassion burn brightly. But that's not, finally, what resulted.

Instead, he confirmed not the grandeur but the twilight of the gods. Reverberations; echoes; ripples; nostalgia. He thought the world could take—at least one more time—visitations from Olympus. But he erred thrice. His men and women were not from Olympus, but from the 19th century, dilated a little by O'Neill's own terrible compulsion to free himself of personal torment; embellished a little by popular literary, psychiatric, and European affectations; stretched somewhat by the ponderous perils they were placed in—but not from Olympus. He erred also because

the 20th century, with its inherent skepticisms and disenchantments, the blows to its social and political pride, its
more scientific assessments of the true frailty and depen-
dence of man, simply wasn't the place for supermen, no
matter how packaged, no matter how briefly impressive
they may seem in the midst of theatrical spasms under
effulgent stage lighting. "The age of heroes," a social critic
observed recently, "like the age of the gods, is dead. It is
time that the age of men began." In truth, it began a long
time ago. Back in the caves, I think. It went unnoticed by
O'Neill through most of his career. When he learned it, as
has already been suggested, it was almost too late.

O'Neill erred, thirdly, because he created an aesthetic
contradiction that he could not resolve. Having established
the fate-ridden, self-destructive, futile—or, in other words,
the *absurd* nature of man, it was hard to prove that absurdity, like cleanliness, was next to godliness. As a consequence, the plays of his productive first period come off
strangely like a doughnut: round, firm, meaty, and well
cooked—but with a hole in the middle. Thirty years later,
when the professional Absurdists come to town, they
brought their own contradiction, and hole, with them; we'll
glance briefly at them later.

Finally, is there a salient, single image of O'Neill? There
is, but not the one he intended. He had hoped to be a
Visionary, a Conscience, a Philosophical Gadfly, a Realist,
a Naturalist, a Social Redeemer, a Cultural Historian, a
Truth-seeker, and a Cosmic Force. He tried all these roles,
sometimes with considerable success. But his real image
isn't in the list. O'Neill, I think, will be remembered most
as the last in the line of American Romantic playwrights,
steeped, inescapably, in the tradition of Herne, Fitch, and
Belasco. Romantic with a capital "R," of course. If we
don't allow ourselves to be deluded or overawed by the
thick psychologizing and philosophical platitudinizing

that burdened so many of his works, we find a Romantic: a man who strips down to his aesthetic birthday suit, pinches his nose, and plunges into the deepest pools of life's agonies and ecstasies, as much to enjoy the sheer rapture of soaking in such pleasures as to proclaim their relevance to man's existence. Presumably allowing the whims of nature to dictate the terms of his art, the Romantic is driven by whatever are the prevailing crosscurrents of thought and style, embracing all with fervor and daring and more than a little awareness of the effect it's having on others. A Romantic may be, at times, deeply pessimistic, but for all O'Neill's storming, his nay-saying, his torment, he could never fully conceal his fundamental *awe,* his irresistible love of the spectacle of life. Nor did he try. He might have been a better playwright if he had.

This is the crux of the matter, the solid but paradoxical contribution to the theatre by O'Neill. It wasn't his plays. It was the image of a man possessed by visions of the monumental frailties of men, but who lacked the dramaturgic skill and the objective discipline to render the visions with universal clarity. O'Neill triumphed, but largely as a vivid symbol of American writers whose dreams have always been mightier than their pens.

Writing with the deepest sense of tribute to the man and the playwright, Joseph Wood Krutch made an astute observation about O'Neill. He was making reference to *Mourning Becomes Electra,* but his remarks apply as well to virtually all of O'Neill's plays. Krutch wrote:

> Here is a scenario to which the most soaring eloquence and the most profound poetry are appropriate. Here also is a treatment of that situation imaginative enough to prepare the spectator to accept language as elevated and as moving as any a dramatic poet ever found. If the language came, we should be swept aloft as no

Anglo-Saxon audience since Shakespeare's time has had an opportunity to be. But no such language does come. . . . That is the penalty we must pay for living in an age whose most powerful dramatist cannot rise above prose.

O'Neill, then, was pound-foolish in dramatic power but penny-wise in poetic diction. He could not, with such an unbalanced artistic budget, revive Tinker Bell.

iii

The Loud, Small Voice of the Poet

Joseph Wood Krutch's lament over an unpoetic O'Neill is a melancholy echo of questions that constantly plague the 20th-century American theatre: Where are the poets hiding, and why don't they come out and save the theatre?

Assuming there are poets, why are they hiding and who (or what) drove them there? Assuming they are lured into the open, why should an artistically mordant and economically hysterical legitimate theatre interest them? Assuming poets can adjust to the barbarities of the professional stage, are they willing to take on the big job: to make great verse once again compatible with great drama?

Poets have good reasons for hiding, and even better ones for leaving the theatre to its own clumsy devices. As for the big job, there's not much that poets can do about it themselves. Indeed, the whole issue of poetry in the theatre is rooted in the peculiarly unsettling nature of a poet's service to contemporary society.

A poet is one of the great anachronisms of the 20th century. His profession cannot be classified with the ease and accuracy of, say, a typewriter repairman or a data processor. He cannot reduce global poverty, criminal activity, or baldness. He cannot package his product and make it attractive through depth psychology probes into human desires or eye-arresting colors that leap off the market shelf. He cannot even—as he used to—instruct us on the delicacies of lovemaking; too many ex-office girls, trained physiologists, and enlightened clergymen seem to do that better, or at least get more popular coverage when they try.

In an era charged by the atmosphere of journalists and technical writers, by poll-takers and statisticians, by the vulgarization of the language in the hands of advertisers, politicians, and garden-variety parents, the poet finds it hard to breathe. Hard enough, in fact, that for tax and census purposes he usually must relabel himself as a "writer"—a safer, if more ambiguous, designation—or to identify with greater precision how he earns his money (usually as a visiting lecturer under a university subsidy, the modern equivalent to the patronage of princes).

To my knowledge, only three American poets—none of whom ever had any direct connection with the theatre—ever made a living writing poetry: Carl Sandburg, Robert Frost, and Ogden Nash. For the rest—and there are many —they must be content with the ephemeral esteem of an occasionally produced "slim volume of verse"; an infrequent Guggenheim (if they can get some verse published first); or, if they're lucky, a "Collected Works of . . ." at a time of life when worldly vanities and pleasures have foresworn the poet, or when he is dead.

It's not my intention to revive the hoary and romantic picture of the poet as a sorrowful, starving waif knocking unheard on the door of mankind, suffering by candlelight in his garret or by sunlight on the ocean front of Big Sur. These quaint pictures are gone. So is the image of Bunthorne, that transparent parody of Oscar Wilde in Gilbert & Sullivan's *Patience*—the "very aesthetical, super-poetical, out-of-the-way young man." Both the underfed, and the overdelicate conceptions have evaporated, and we can be very grateful.

No matter how much compassion we may have for the thankless and unrewarded tribulations of the poet, we'd do him a terrible disservice by romanticizing his function. When we make such a mistake, we are falsifying our expectations and obscuring the essential meaning of poetry. We are still very guilty of such falsifying and obscuring—a result, perhaps, of the inherited Romantic tradition with its spectacle of the raw, passionate soul of the poet spilling over before our eyes in cascades of effulgent and heady metaphors. So numbing an experience is it, that we often prefer to wallow in style rather than substance, to subvert the pivotal Truth the poet is trying to pronounce in favor of self-indulgent rhapsodizing over lyrical power, stunning conceits of language, or emotion-charged imagery.

But it's not the Romantic tradition alone that is most responsible for our misconstruing the poet's real service to humanity. There's a deeper, and simpler, reason. The poet, no matter what his disposition toward his world or toward his art, is a dangerous man; and a dangerous man is always, as I suggested earlier, an anachronism in any society that is trying to cultivate safe and stable virtues. Indeed, the poet would be the last to qualify for the Boy Scout oath.

He is not "helpful." To cut into the bedrock, the human mantle of calcified ideas and emotions, he needs complex tools: irony, ambiguity, metaphor, metrics, cadence. He is not obliged to explain or defend these tools, any more than a plumber or carpenter must explain his. So, on the surface, at least, the poet seems bent on confounding us, on dimming, rather than brightening his objectives.

He is not "friendly" or "kind." In fact, by the very nature of his work, the poet is a supremely ruthless man, subjecting ideas, images, and words to the most despotic reformations. The tautness of the single line, the stringent measuring out of syllables, the meticulous weighting of rhyme sequences are severe disciplines that seem to free *him,* but alarm us. Normal human beings tend to blanket their sorrows, embellish their joys, multiply their anxieties; but the poet can't allow himself these indulgences. He must carve and hack away at all the digressive and discursive tactics that are used to substitute the practices of living for the reality of life. His efforts to discover an absolute standard of expression for recording his experiences makes him appear, superficially, to be a poor prospect as a house guest.

He is not "courteous" or "loyal"—certainly not in the conventional meanings of these terms. To be either, or both, would suggest that he has accepted certain moral codes that are contrary to his nature; codes that would, indeed, destroy him. He can live in no one's terms but his own, so that he doesn't imperil the critical distance he must maintain from the tumultuous stream of everyday vanities and customs.

This release from the customary standards and preoccupations is not license for indiscriminate nonconformity. He knows his role and responsibilities too well to waste his time and exhaust himself in this manner. He knows that though the terms of his vision must remain uniquely his own, he isn't the other side of the humanoid coin; he is its thickness; he is the sharpness of relief into which the imprinted figure is thrown. He is the *value* of the coin. Questions of courtesy and loyalty may help the average man justify his conscience or build up Green Stamps for heaven—but the poet reserves the right to be courteous and loyal only to the vision of the potential beauty or awesome truth about all men.

So the poet is unhelpful, unfriendly, unkind, discourteous, disloyal, and so forth. That's fine. I don't want his feet stuck in my syrupy platitudes. But it does help to underscore why—by desire, by necessity, and by nature—he seems at times like an outlander, a foreigner admitted when we weren't watching the gate too carefully. And because we have the peculiar, egoistic habit of making ourselves the center of the universe, we invariably tend to use ourselves as a point of reference in making judgments about poetry and poets. When we do this—as we always do—we are irritated and unsettled by the results of the comparison. Because the poet is more vulnerable to life's impressions than we are, he makes us conscious of being cheated; because he is more selective in his ideas, we are unnerved by the flaccidity of our thinking; because he is better disciplined in imposing order on his feelings, we are distressed by the clumsiness of our own authority over strong emotions; because he is more facile in the use of language, we are dismayed by the ponderous, tongue-tied nature of our own verbal equipment; because he is, finally, more perceptive of life's disorders, ambiguities, and essential pleasures, we are made envious and are mortified by our own density and blindness.

These are hardly very positive, reassuring reactions. Imagine, then, if you will, feedback of this kind occurring during the performance of a play, and you will begin to imagine why audiences are made very restless by poetry in the theatre. Poets and poetry, as supreme phenomena of civilized man, seem peculiarly remote. Perhaps it's not all the fault of poets. To be entirely fair to them, therefore, and to deepen the perspective on the climate for poetry in which the theatre is obliged to exist, we'll leave poets for a moment and shift to you.

(Incidentally, it's surely becoming abundantly clear even now that poets and the theatre are doomed to a wholly incompatible relationship in the 20th century. Or so it would seem. The relationship is rather like that of parents and children: you can't live with them, and you get lonely without them.)

What does the "poetic experience" mean to most of us? Not too much, really. Our contacts with it are sporadic, tentative, inadequate.

For many, this contact may extend no further than the few pedestrian couplets we have to choke down when we buy a greeting card, or to tolerate indulgently as our child practices a "piece" for a school assembly program. It may extend beyond, to those framed verses sentimentalizing mother-love or babyhood that we still find, occasionally, hanging on living room walls. Contact may have been made through those sticky platitudes that versifiers the likes of James J. Metcalf and Edgar Guest used to syndicate to newspapers, offering, like spiritual Alka-Seltzer, a quick pick-me-up and instant relief from cultural heartburn. Contact may even extend to the writing of some verse ourselves, usually perpetrated just on the far side of puberty and invariably as a covert activity. Normally such verses mortify us when discovered years later; not because the verses are bad—which they probably were—but because we are intimidated by a different and lost part of ourselves that dared to express its most urgent feelings.

Contact with poetry was bound to occur in school. If you were lucky, your teacher was utterly opaque on the subject and left poetry alone. But state laws, unfortunately, prevented her from doing that. If you were only somewhat lucky, your teacher badgered you with iambics, dactyls, and trochees. The more cunning teacher might even have coerced you into identifying a *caesura* or the gratuitous distinction between the Italian and Shakespearean sonnet. Such badgering and coercing wasn't all bad; it did develop the "Thump and Pound Recitation School of Poetic Appreciation":

> His *back against* a *rock* he *bore*
> And *firmly placed* his *foot before*
> "Come *one*, come *all*, this *rock* shall *fly*
> From *its* form *base* as *soon* as *I.*"

Your contact was *least* fortunate if your teacher was

bred in the tradition of Romantic poetry—as many still are—and was trained in college by professors of literature whose minds have become trapped in the trough between Beowulf and Thomas Hardy. Basically, there's nothing wrong, of course, with Romantic poetry, literature professors or Beowulf—except that in sluggish and distracted minds they create wrong impressions of poetry, which easily becomes misconstrued as an ornament of society, as rapturous inspiration, as a helpless cadaver waiting for the dissecting blade; in other words, poetry that is treated as a phenomenon essentially unrelated to the hard, incessant mainstream of human dream and endeavor.

It's no wonder that poets of the 20th century have made precipitous nosedives into esoteric cubbyholes, pulling their similes and metaphors in after them. Imagists, Surrealists, Symbolists, and Expressionists have hastened the retreat of the poet from society, moving into tight cliques and private coteries, writing in a kind of insular shorthand that only the initiated and a handful of literary critics could decipher. I don't blame them. Poetry—as a mass experience, as a fundamental diet of a human culture—is so alien to the American experience, so rejected, that poets, to protect the sacred endowments, have had to draw into circles, like Custer's troops, to fight off the Indians. It should have been a commonplace event to find an old poet sharing the dias with a young president. Conditions being what they are, however, it was a shocker.

For a long time I thought that my hostility toward the treatment of poetry in the schools was the result of a strictly personal experience. My teachers were no more nor no less exhausted or distracted by years of underpaid, underappreciated labor. But I do remember that they *read* poetry very badly. That's an ominous and revealing sign, I realized later; even the ones with good voices read badly. And I think the reason was twofold: they disliked it and were afraid of it. Disliked it because they didn't understand the powerful, germinal impulse that precipitates a poem into being in the first place; afraid of it because to retrace that impulse to its origin, as Stephen Spender once insisted we have to do, is an arduous and frustrating task, forcing us to reveal the imperfections in our own critical and emotional perceptions. Perhaps they were also afraid of offending the masculine image inherent in American democracy by displaying a taste for the refined, elegant, and delicate.

They were bad readers and I hated them for it and for what they were doing to countless unsuspecting souls who might have found something likable, immediate, and necessary in poetry. (Interestingly, it was a German teacher, Miss Wyman, who kept my enchantment more or less intact. She used to read Heine, in German—although we were hardly ready for it—with such tenderness of feeling, such radiance of spirit, with such an awesome clarity and nuance of expression, that I began to realize what a civil, civilizing, and courageous act it was to love and honor poetry.)

Contact doesn't stop in high school, of course. College invariably has its own devices for stamping out what little love and honor are left. The notion that poetry is decoration is gone, of course; it's too immature a concept. But another one is substituted: poetry as the sharpening stone for the intellectual bravura of the instructor, for his brilliant lint-picking, for the display of the protean jargon that has been developed that ostensibly "explains" everything about a poem—everything, that is, except why poetry fails to move and excite us, except why poetry must feed off itself to be understood instead of feeding off a universal fund of human experience, except why the poet is obliged to hide behind "objective correlatives," "seven forms of ambiguity," and "attenuated metaphors."

What both the high school and college poetic experience

usually have in common is the peculiar notion that a poem, once printed and once sanctified by the critical gods, is an inert, finished thing. Its life is over; it lays there, supine and vulnerable, fair game for whatever are the prevailing prejudices, fallibilities, or popular intellectual fashions; anthologized and reanthologized; prefaced, footnoted, and historically documented. But remaining, ultimately, in the hands of the chosen.

That a poem might represent only an interim resolution to the problem of form and content, only a partial and still searching answer, merely the tentative illumination of an active encounter with life, seems to escape most of us. That a poem, like living protoplasm, continues to divide and subdivide its cells, pressing at the thin walls of form that are trying to contain them, seems, at times, only secondary. And as long as it remains secondary, poetry will persist in its role as something faintly alien, exotic, unconnected with the realities of existence, and very out of place in the theatre.

I don't know who is most at fault for this condition—poets themselves who are legitimately discouraged by the sullen response of the general public and are thus obliged to write for other poets, or the professional critics and scholars who see an opportunity for vested interests in this condition and cherish the role of oracles, writing their cogent critiques and analyses for other critics and scholars. It's a wicked circle.

Well, contact with poetry is likely to continue after college, but it's too embarrassing to go into. Books reviewed by ladies' clubs are rarely books of poetry. ("I'm not really equipped to explain it, my dear.") Readings of their own works by any but the most famous of practicing poets are, as a rule, sparsely attended, and then largely by literature majors and local versemakers. Where verse today is the most abundant is, of course, on television where the notion of "Masscult" has debased poetry into driving, jingly stanzas that try to pound deodorants and margarines into our heads. (It's revolting, naturally, but it's honest. At least commercial-makers recognize the primitive desires that can be aroused by the strong rhythmic pulse and vivid imagery of verse.)

I suspect that a few of us have made deliberate efforts to avoid contact with poetry. Not with novels; you may have purchased three to five books in the past twelve months. Not with music; I'm sure you've added to your record collection and attended a fair number of concerts. (It's curious: although music is considered virtually the ultimate in abstract, symbolic communication, employing tones that have no literal meaning or harmonic developments that are more mathematically precise than the average brain can fathom, music enjoys a far more widespread popularity than does poetry.) You may even have attended a few plays, although box office figures for anything but musicals and touring, warmed-over Broadway successes are dismaying.

Now the obvious and loaded question: how many books of verse have you purchased in the past twelve months? To protect you—and me—I'll let that stand as a rhetorical question because, in truth, it may not even be a fair one.

It's a patent paradox, isn't it? At a time when technology breeds affluence, and affluence breeds leisure, and leisure breeds contemplation, and contemplation breeds—or ought to—deeper assessments of what we're doing meandering around this alien planet, those acknowledged spokesmen of man's durability, and of his capacity to live with and be proud of himself, are unheard, unread, and unbought.

This is no accusation, no effort to intimidate a captive audience. I suspect I'm as guilty as the rest of not supporting, reading, and buying good verse with the regularity and enthusiasm that I should. But I think I've learned something from my own inadequacy: the Great Public Guilts that writers have identified after surveying the range of everyday disasters—the *mea culpa* syndrome that Arthur Miller, for example, enjoys displaying so much— are really limited in scope, limited in vision because they deal only with the tangible corruptions of living: social, political, and religious crimes; the crises that man encounters as he tries to protect himself or enlarge his personal interests. But there is a much greater and deeper guilt at work, and this takes the form of cultural self-betrayal.

If man is the microcosm, the embodiment of all those ultimate abstractions of good and evil, of all those shimmering promises for self-directed greatness; if he represents the uneasy synthesis of primitive and civilized traits; if one man is truly *all men*—and he'd *better* be, or all religions, all social institutions, and all art collapses—then he is not only a natural target for poetry, he is *himself* a *poetic idea*. Thus, all the controversy, all the niggling scholasticisms, all the pretentious gabble by critics and professors, all the widely proclaimed schisms that seem to exist between the poet and the so-called "common man"—are silly. The Greater Guilt lies in our failure, as a civilized, educated, and affluent people, to restore the natural continuity, the inevitable reciprocity that exists between man and his capacity to construct both truthful and idealized images of himself.

The absence of this continuity has been aggravated because too few people have the patience to at least touch, if not dig out, the roots of our terrible inertia in the matter of theatre poetry. We've labored far too long the notions of the economic unfeasibility of poetic drama, of the poor equipment of American actors to speak verse well, of the poverty of American audiences to hear and savor good verse. I suspect these arguments; I smell evasive tactics. Poetic plays *have* been produced with success; actors *can* be trained to speak well; American audiences are *not* stupid, though they often don't know it.

Perhaps if we document this dilemma a little more concretely with reference to something of what has actually happened on the American stage, we might be in a better position to judge what has been accomplished, and why it never seems to be enough.

Writing in *The New York Times* back in 1935, Maxwell Anderson—who was once held to be the chief apostle and great white hope of theatre poetry—remarked:

> We shall not always be as we are—but what we are to become depends on what we dream and desire. The theatre, more than any other art, has the power to weld and determine what the race dreams into what the race will become. All this may sound rather farfetched in the face of our present Broadway . . . but Broadway is itself as transient as the real-estate values under its feet. Those of us who fail to outlive the street in which we work will fail because we have accepted its valuations and measured our product by them.

In retrospect, it's a sorrowful statement. Anderson failed to outlive the street, and its valuations not only tainted his work deeply—to the disappointment of many—but colored him altogether.

I cite his remarks, though, because they serve as well as any to enunciate, a little plaintively, the battle cry of theatre versemakers, a cry that reverberates deep into the past and continues to be heard to the present. And like most of the plaintive cries, they reflect the failure of poetry to weld the racial dream with the racial reality. We'll return to Anderson shortly.

The story of poetic drama in the United States is, in the words of one critic, "the story of occasional conquest in the face of gigantic frustration." This frustration is all the more frustrating in view of the great flowering of poetry and prose in 19th-century New England and a national renascence in virtually all the arts that began around 1915.

But the dramatic poet was not, unfortunately, offered a seat at this festive table. At about the time of the Armory Show, in which academic art was buried under a vital wave of European experiment in painting and sculpture, the nearest thing to poetry on the American professional stage was *The Merry Widow* and Edward Sheldon's (remember him—of *Margaret Fleming* fame?) pseudorealistic *Romance* starring Doris Keane.

It's really no surprise that poets have been uncomfortable in the marketplace of the theatre. Where even a tentative jointure was made, the results were usually ill fated. Poets have squirmed under the impediments that theatre normally imposes on any writer. That's as it should be, I suppose.

The theatre demands intensity, clarity, velocity. The poet has often preferred to muse, to murmur subtle ironies, to impede the action by brilliant excursions into sonorous images that delight the ear but bore the body.

Producers, on their side, have had little use for such unprofitable commodities as the Sublime or the Eloquent. We can't blame them either. Producers have their own special kind of racial memory, and they are especially transfixed by the memory of the unquenchable bombast that posed as poetry for most of the 19th century and the formidable "elocutionists" who used to recite it.

The only occasion when a common ground develops is when the word "poetry" has the broadest, most flexible definition. When poetry means the maximum compression of universally understood experience, embodied in strong emotional images drawn from familiar occurrences and beliefs—almost any good dramatist can join the club, from Robinson Jeffers to Arthur Miller, from Archibald Mac-

Leish to Tennessee Williams. But then is it poetry any more? Yes, indeed. It took T. S. Eliot nearly thirty years to come around to recognizing that, for the theatre, it's not meter, rhyme, or structure that really matters. What does matter, finally, is the symbolic force that each character represents, the stylistically unique form of utterance each is given, and the careful delineation of the rhythmic impulse that underscores their actions. If you keep this broad definition in mind, there may be, ultimately, an opportunity to rejoin the human race with human dreams.

Earlier I promised a "story" of poetic drama in the American theatre. I think I've hedged on the promise because the story starts off so badly.

It begins in 1767 with a performance at the Southwark Theatre in Philadelphia of Thomas Godfrey's *The Prince of Parthia*. The author, who had the bad grace to die four years earlier, never got to see this turgid, bloody, unyielding epic of love, lust, passion, honor, and death. The plot is of no account. If you know *Hamlet, Romeo and Juliet, Julius Caesar, Macbeth,* and Beaumont's *The Maid's Tragedy,* and stir them all together robustly, you know what *The Prince of Parthia* is about. One major theatre historian refers to the language of the play as "dignified." I will grant it that. In dignified blank verse it begins:

> He comes, Arsaces comes, my gallant brother
> (Like shining Mars in all the pomp of conquest)
> Triumphant enters now our joyful gates;
> Bright Victory waits on his glitt'ring ear,
> And shows her fav'rite to the wond'ring croud;
> While Fame exulting sounds the happy name
> To realms remote, and bids the world admire.
> Oh! 't is a glorious day:—let none presume
> T' indulge the tear, or wear the gloom of sorrow;
> This day shall shine in Ages yet to come,
> And grace the PARTHIAN story.

If you have endured the hammering pentameters of the opening address, you may survive until one of the high points of the play, in Act III, scene 7, when court skulduggery is threatening to separate "shining Mars" (the hero, Arsaces) from his true love, Evanthe. Arsaces erupts with:

> Ha! will he force thee from me?
> What, tear thee from my fond and bleeding heart?
> And must I lose thee ever? dreadful word!
> Never to gaze upon thy beauties more?
> Never to taste the sweetness of thy lips?
> Never to know the joys of mutual love?
> Never—! Oh! let me lose the pow'r of thinking,
> For thought is near allied to desperation.
> Why, cruel sire—why did you give me life,
> And load it with a weight of wretchedness?
> Take back my being, or relieve my sorrows—
> Ha! art thou not Evanthe?—Art thou
> not the lovely Maid, who bless'd the fond
> Arsaces? (Raving)

Evanthe forces herself to answer: "Alas! I fear your senses are unsettled!"

It's too easy to ridicule what was evidently an earnest and not untalented effort to bring a classical power and decorum to the American stage. We needed it badly. But by reconstructing the mythical and exotic kingdom of Parthia, Godfrey indulged himself in a kind of romantic escapism as a device to justify the grand passions and windy oratory of the play. This retreat device has always been popular: Sophocles, Shakespeare, and Goethe used it, to name just three. Anderson, Jeffers, and MacLeish used it, to name three more. And it's a good device, *provided* it is used as an immaterial and transparent skeleton that can be fleshed out with the dramatic idiom and intellectual imperatives of the playwright's *own* day. American writers have not been uniformly skilled at this, certainly not as clever as the French (Anouilh, Giraudoux, Cocteau, and Sartre).

What Godfrey launched—the self-conscious bombast emanating from overidealized settings and language—was to be a persistent and crippling convention for the next seventy-five to eighty years. William Dunlap's *Andre,* James Nelson Barker's *Superstition,* Robert Montgomery Bird's *The Broker of Bogota,* Nathaniel Parker Willis' *Tortesa the Usurer*—even though some used American settings—all convey an emotional exuberance and stylistic detachment that make them unconvincing records of human experience.

Matters changed somewhat in 1855 with the appearance of George Henry Boker's *Francesca da Rimini.* Here again was the remote locale, the borrowed legend (this time from Dante's *Inferno*) and the elevated oratory—but with a difference. The ill-fated love triangle involving Lanciotto, the bold but deformed warrior; Paolo, his handsome brother; and Francesca, the idealized Renaissance beauty on whose acceptance of Lanciotto hangs the peace and honor of two kingdoms, is conventional enough. The language is organized in the usual unrhymed iambic pentameter; the passions are, as usual, towering. But we detect something new: a serious effort by the author to suppress, reduce, and fragmentize the normally rigid structure of the verse in order to strengthen the individuality of character and the dramatic thrust of the scene. The lofty similes are gone, with all their pseudomythological overtones, the meter is regularly abandoned to permit the small and large peculiarities and aches of the people to come through.

When his father commands him to marry the beautiful Francesca, Lanciotto is stunned into revealing a painful truth about himself:

> what, I—
> Ho! I have found my use at last—
> What. I. (Laughing)
> I, the great twisted monster of the wars,
> The brawny cripple, the herculean dwarf,
> The spur of panic, and the butt of scorn—
> I be a bridegroom! Heaven, was I not cursed
> More than enough, when thou didst fashion me
> To be a type of ugliness—a thing
> By whose comparison all Rimini
> Holds itself beautiful? Lo! here I stand,
> A gnarled, blighted trunk! There's not a knave
> So spindle-shanked, so wry-faced, so infirm,
> Who looks at me, and smiles not on himself.

Now you're witnessing a man in distress rather than a poet in a spasm. The verse is easy, softer, more capable of molding itself to the specific desire of the man who feels. The imagery is strong, but wholly appropriate. The irony is powerful, but it derives from the frightening notion of a "blighted trunk" becoming a bridegroom.

In the final moments of the play, the full resources of Boker's dramatic and poetic skills are brought to bear. Lanciotto begs his brother to lie to him, demands it, so that he can avoid the truth of Paolo's and Francesca's love affair, and thus avoid what the code of personal honor requires: the killing of both. But Paolo refuses; to compound the dishonor would be unthinkable. And so both are killed, more in despair than in rage. Lanciotto's final words are steeped in bitter melancholy. Notice how the language breaks and bends into the contour of the man's personal sorrow, how the cadence becomes alternately transparent and opaque as the emotions shift abruptly, how free and responsive the metrics are to the needs of a man in great spiritual pain:

> I will to the wars,
> And do more murders to eclipse this one.

Back to the battles; there I breathe in peace;
And I will take a soldier's honour back.—
Honour! what's that to me now? Ha!
    ha! ha!
A great thing, father! I am very ill.
I killed thy son for honor: thou mayst chide.
O God! I cannot cheat myself with words!
I loved him more than honour—more than life—
This man, my Paolo—this stark, bleeding corpse!
Here let me rest, till God awake us all!

Poetic matters remained pretty sparse for the rest of the century. Poe and Longfellow took flyers at writing poetic drama but, like Thomas Hardy in England, their works proved unstageworthy. It was a man with the reputation for writing potboilers who gave the 20th-century theatre a small poetic impetus. The man was William Vaughan Moody, really better known for his hair-curling melodrama, *The Great Divide,* one of the first plays to foreshadow the epic drama of life in the American Far West. While satisfying the commercial theatre with pseudorealistic thrillers, he was trying to complete a remarkable trilogy, based on biblical legend. He called the three parts *The Fire-Bringer, The Masque of Judgement,* and *The Death of Eve.* The plays failed to find an audience, which is unfortunate because the audience then did not get to enjoy one of the minor milestones in the evolution of a verse form that was beginning to approach that delicate balance between fact and melody. To suggest something of Moody's skill in weaving supple, fragile, and speakable imagery through traditional five-beat, blank verse lines, here is a sample of his dramatic verse:

There was a day when winter held the hills
And all the lower places looking sunward
Knew that spring was near. Until that day
I had but walked in a boy's dream and dazzle,

And in soft darkness folded on herself
My soul had spun her blind and silken house.
It was my birthday, for at earliest dawn
You had crept to me in the outer tent,
Kissed me with tears and laughter, whispering low
That I was born, and that the world was there,
A gift you had imagined and made for me.

The purple passions are gone. The lines flow, without impedence, almost like rich prose. The sense of revery, love, and myth transcend the words themselves, accomplishing what the devices of any good artistic medium try to accomplish: the elimination of themselves in favor of a superior impression. The sense of wonder, in other words, is infinitely more paramount than the machinery of the verse. Moody was beginning to demonstrate that not the interior rhythms, not the external technique, not the management of figures of speech, not a self-conscious "poetizing" are the essential goals of good stage poetry. Moody knew—as many other writers did not—that the magic of verse is to free, not encumber, a strong human idea. To "point to" an idea and not get in its way, as Eliot suggested. It was a belief he never got a chance to prove to the paying public.

Edna St. Vincent Millay, however, did find a public, but she had to cavort, play the fool, and borrow heavily from the traditions of the commedia dell'arte to do it. Adopting a verse form that was virtually promiscuous in its freeness, and poorly concealing a cutting piece of pacifist propaganda, she created a delicate masterpiece in *Aria da Capo*. Here, the whimsical figures of the Italian Comedy, Pierrot and Columbine, are used as a framework—rather like book-ends—for a bucolic scene beween two shepherds. The men seemed to be engaged in harmless discussion about drinking water and jewels, when the atmosphere begins to shift and we discover that they have become microcosms of warring nations, each trying to out-smart and destroy the other. The scene turns tragic as the shepherds kill one another. Pierrot and Columbine, totally immune to the spectacle of death and destruction, roll the corpses under their banquet table and close the play the way they began it—with the same pointless, trivial banter:

COL: Pierrot, a macaroon! I cannot *live* without a macaroon!

PIER: My only love,
You are so intense! Is it Tuesday, Columbine? I'll kiss you if it's Tuesday!

COL: It is Wednesday,
If you must know . . . Is this my artichoke? Or Yours?

The elegant pacifism of Millay was not an especially popular viewpoint among theatre poets of the 1930's. The Spanish Civil War produced another, and more activist, philosophy that found a spokesman in Archibald MacLeish. Committed to the philosophy that pacifism is but another form of moral debasement, that merely to remain alienated from the great thrust of political change and revolution is the equivalent of being dead—a notion Bertolt Brecht would extend in great depth—MacLeish turned to the forum of the stage. The stage turned out to be the epoch-making but short-lived Columbia Radio Workshop of 1937.

For his special brand of protest, MacLeish created a verse drama entitled *The Fall of the City,* a bitter portrait of an unnamed people in an unidentified country in which the citizens are so *willing* to be enslaved that they create their own tyrant.

Using the "You Are There" approach that was to become so vital a radio broadcasting device later on, MacLeish sets an "on-the-spot" commentator in the midst of the ten thousand or more people crowded into the city square. A powerful undercurrent of terror permeates the mob. They cry out, begging for a master, someone who will rule them, enchain them. Then the announcer speaks:

> Now there's a sound. They see him. They must see him!
> They're shading their eyes from the sun: there's a
>   rustle of whispering:
> We can't see for the glare of it . . . Yes! Yes!
> He's there in the end of the street in the shadow.
>   We see him!
> He looks huge—a head taller than anyone:
> Broad as a brass door: a hard hero:
> Heavy of heel on the brick: clanking with metal:
> The helm closed on his head: the eyeholes hollow.
> He's coming!
>   He's clear of the shadows! . . .
>   The sun takes him.
> They cover their faces with fingers. They cower
>   before him.
> They fall: they sprawl on the stone. He's alone
>   where he's walking.
> He marches with rattle of metal. He tramples his
>   shadow.
> He mounts by the pyramid—stamps on the stairway
>   —turns—
> His arm rises—his visor is opening. . . .
>   There's no one! . . .
> There's no one at all!
>   No one!
>   The helmet is hollow!
> The metal is empty! The armor is empty! I tell you
> There's no one at all there; there's only the metal:
> The barrel of metal; the bundle of armor. It's empty.

I'm sure you detected the essential power of such verse:

the harsh rat-tat-tat cadence, the emotional jolts created by tense phrases, the vivid action imagery ("sprawls," "marches," "tramples," "mounts," "stamps"), and the strong force of the colloquial language. An effective piece, to be sure, especially when considered as a problem in creating good radio drama; that is, to create dynamic pictures through words alone. It's especially effective when you also realize what is not readily apparent—that he was using the hoary iambic pentameter line again, still the trusty servant of natural human speech patterns.

What MacLeish was attempting, apparently, was what Henry James once claimed he was obliged to do when he sailed into the theatre as a poet: to "eliminate the cargo in order to save the ship." In other words, to provide "instant" poetry; that kind of experience that would brew up, like powdered coffee, into a fast, aromatic experience, providing quick, uncomplicated satisfactions by appealing to the most easily pronounced appetites: pounding rhythms, raw and colloquial images, startling dramatic turns. This is not wrong or bad. Even if it were, it wouldn't be in the hands of a distinguished poet like MacLeish. Yet even he confesses that, because an audience is so conscious of poetry *as* poetry when they watch and hear a play in verse, poetry is often a dramatic liability to the poet, that it "gets in the way of the dramatic action."

What to do about this dilemma? MacLeish has no final answer, although he did suggest once that at least part of the fault lies in the basic conception we have of what the theatre is supposed to show: life as it is, or life as it could be. Presently, our expectations are so strong for hearing words spoken on the stage that we might have heard spoken in our living rooms that when the poet wants to write for the theatre he must either (1) hide the fact that he's a poet, or (2) turn magician and display a prop-box full of cunning tricks and disguises so that he can completely alter our expectations while revealing his virtuosity as a manipulator of language. There's something vaguely unsettling about having to choose either of these options; but the choice must be made—and it's usually the second —until such time as we can be truly convinced that we are not an "unpoetic" people.

Twenty-two years after *The Fall of the City,* MacLeish made his first formidable attack on the prosaic walls of Broadway with *J. B.* It won him a Pulitzer Prize in 1959— given more as a gesture of gratitude, I think, than as a reward for merit.

It's almost sacrilegious to even hint at the inadequacy of this play. The fact remains, however, that the play fails, even while we cheer the fact that it was written. And it fails for the usual reason: MacLeish is too good a poet and too bad a playwright. The mysterious equation, the secret alchemy that fuses action and language was not discovered by the author. (Maybe it never will be. Maybe it's true, as someone said, that the playwright *thinks* one play and writes a second, the actors find a third, and the audience a fourth—and whatever equation was originally intended is lost.)

But as an exercise in the potentiality and scope of dramatic verse, the play is a wonder, a veritable handbook of the various attitudes a poet can strike. Because it could serve as a textbook for apprentice theatre poets, the play merits a slightly more generous look.

MacLeish demonstrated, for instance, how words could be marshaled into ferocious, satanic sounds, the kind he had Nickles spew from his mouth:

> I taste of the world.
> I've licked the stick that beat my brains out—
> Stock that broke my father's bones.

And later:

> We never asked him to be born.
> We never chose the lives we die of.
> They beat our rumps to make us breathe.
> But God, if we have suffered patiently,
> Borne it in silence, stood the stench,
> Rewards us. Gives us our dirty souls back.

The imagery is appropriately brutal and vulgar; the short, four-beat line has the effect of saber slashes; the calculated repetition of certain consonant sounds—the plosive "b's," the hissing "s," the gutteral "ck"—create emotional lesions in our skin.

A strikingly different effect is achieved in the turkey scene. MacLeish captures the weightless, frivolous banter of children waiting to dig into the feast. The poet skillfully abuses the basic tetrameter line in order to preserve the incandescence of a loving, happy family:

> Papá! Papá! He heard! He heard!
> Who did?
> Ourfatherwhichartinheaven.
> He did indeed. What a bird He sent us!
> Cooked to a turn!
> He heard! He heard!
> He heard! He heard! He sent a bird!
> That's enough now, children. Quiet!
> Your father's counting.
> Not today.
> Not this gobbler. Feed a regiment.

In truth, it's very affecting. Capturing and formalizing the sweet sing-song of children's chatter while still preserving the fundamental credibility of the situation is no mean accomplishment.

Nor is the solemn, hymnlike intoning that MacLeish creates at the end of the play, as Sarah speaks:

> The candles in churches are out.
> The lights have gone out in the sky.
> Blow on the coal of the heart
> And we'll see by and by. . . . .
>   we'll see where we are.
> We'll know. We'll know.

The verse has been squeezed to three beats, but to ensure the breadth and sonority of the sound, MacLeish invokes the nostalgia of an old hymn ("We will meet in the sweet bye and bye") and, even more subtly, stresses the more resonant vowel sounds to underscore the muted nature, the pliancy of spirit, and the forgiving, humbling pose at the end.

A skillful, poetic craftsman, indeed. But despite his craft, or perhaps because of it, he remains a journeyman, an incipient dramatist. The character of J. B. is reduced to a talky and inoperative figure. Sarah, his wife, is virtually a nag, betraying little more than a commonplace acceptance of the tidy *hausfrau* role. Throughout the play there is neither a declaration of or an active search for a positive statement that is faithful to 20th-century man's skeptical attitude toward Jobian suffering; and with characters reduced to laboratory specimens and the theme to an untenable fairy tale, the play shrivels to empty ruminations that give off the odor of piety or sermonizing.

Up to the last page of playscript, to the final three minutes of playing time, MacLeish plays both sides of the street. The repeated blows to his body and soul finally embitter J. B. Hooray. He's mad as the proverbial wet hen. He scorns the Comforters, God, his wife, himself. He's now on the verge—maybe—of trying to articulate, out of this cornucopia of pain and disaster, a fresh vision of the 20th-century's vis-à-vis with God. But MacLeish won't let him do it. Like an expatriate from the Bible Belt, and with the dramatic technique that would shock an undergraduate drama major, he abruptly throws the man and the play into reverse gear with a nine-word stage direction ("Slowly, with difficulty, the hard words said at last.") J. B. falls to his knees, and in fourteen lines of ambiguous, sentimental verse, our hero announces he's willing to start all over again.

Few men have come to the theatre with such brilliant literary equipment as MacLeish. Few have articulated thoughts on the function of the theatre with such cogency and enthusiasm as MacLeish. Few have dared to assault with such freshness of vision one of the more delicate and pervasive myths of contemporary man—namely, the still-strong Christian legend and ethic—and lived to tell about it.

J. B. remains, nonetheless, aesthetically schizoid; a bold poetic idea propelled by inadequate and antiquated dramatic machinery. And because the play represents, in many ways, both the promise and the failure of the poetic theatre in America, its inadequacy is all the more compelling; indeed, even tragic.

MacLeish was not, finally, the synthesizer of dramatic storyteller and lyric phrasemaker. Perhaps a poet with theatrical propensities should not be expected to carry off such a task; perhaps, instead, a legitimate playwright with poetical propensities could do it better. This is what the critics and public thought—and hoped for—in the 1930's, when Maxwell Anderson arrived.

Anderson assumed the job of reuniting poetry and drama with sober assurance. To provide a theoretical basis for his mission, he drew up a new "Poetics" for serious drama that radiated hope, inspiration, and echoes of Aristotle himself. In this document, which he called "The Essence of Tragedy," Anderson flatly rejected prose as a vehicle for serious plays. "Under the strain of an emotion," he insisted, "the ordinary prose of the stage breaks down into inarticulateness, just as it does in life. Hence the cult of understatement, hence the realistic drama in which the climax is reached in an eloquent gesture or a moment of meaningful silence." So, to qualify by Anderson's standards, a dramatist simply *had* to be a poet.

So far, all well and good, if we cling to the freer definition of "poet"; that is, one who is attuned to the deeper melodies and resonances in human experience. But Anderson, through most of his major works, declined to accept such a definition, preferring to "saw the air" with words; feverishly, illogically, and often pointlessly dragging in bombastic rhetoric that might have served as a model for *Prince of Parthia*. (I'm not, incidentally, merely trying to align myself with those skeptical, cerebral critics who are impatient with phony puffing, or with any concept of aesthetic obsolescence. The vacuity of Anderson's verse, its dripping overripeness, its fundamental incompatibility with the variety and subtlety of characters he tried to create—all this was detected, examined, and mourned over in the 1940's, as soon as he had shifted, thankfully, back into prose. Indeed, I have been as innocently and helplessly drawn into plays such as *Winterset* and *Elizabeth the Queen* as anyone, gotten all choked up, perspired. Later I realized that these were plays for very young people, for undiluted Romantics, willing to forego reason in favor of rapture, intelligence for inspiration, craftsmanship for emotional concussions.)

So Anderson wrote a doctrine, demanding that the playwright be a poet; that the working mainspring of a modern play be triggered by a discovery on the part of the hero of something in him or in his environment that he was not aware of before; that the discovery be the high point of the play, radically affecting the thought and direction of the hero; that the hero be imperfect and learn his shortcomings through suffering. If he suffers enough, he will be spiritually reawakened.

Fair proposals, indeed. It would have made Aristotle, who proposed them first, very proud. It's a shame Anderson didn't heed them.

At least he had zeal, a commodity noticeably lacking in many professionals, and an earnest desire to improve the American theatre by trying to reproduce another Elizabethan era. But it didn't work.

Take *Winterset*, for example. A good example, really, because it was based, as we know, on a contemporary event (the Sacco-Vanzetti business) and is set in a contemporary environment. The problem the play represents is simply this: Can the sordid business of a modern revenge story be properly enhanced by dramatic verse? Yes, obviously—if it remains a fierce, unswerving search for vengeance. (Possibly providing a wonderfully exhilarating antidote to modern life and to all the temporizing and compromising this life demands of us—when we'd really prefer to go out— like a Western hero—and gun the villain down.) The actual answer, however, was no. The heart has its mysteries, I suppose, and so do playwrights. By some facile heart-pumping that would do credit to *Redbook* and *True Romances*, he proves that the power of young love can turn a thirst for vengeance into a maudlin melodrama of forgiveness. (There's *Margaret Fleming* still hovering around.)

Anderson's other major poetic efforts—*Masque of Kings, Mary of Scotland,* and *Elizabeth the Queen*—despite a number of glorious interludes of verse that have a melting simplicity, remain masquerades of overdressed mannequins breathing labored, pretentious words that do more to stifle human passions than to reveal them.

It would seem, then, that the matter is hopeless; that verse as a medium of theatrical expression is a dormant, if not dead, issue; that good poets are poor playwrights; that good playwrights are poor poets. This, of course, is not the case. We might, however, mourn the fact that the so-called "social realists" continue in power, hammering at us with deadening prose until we're ready to turn in our ears and sell our imaginations. We might also mourn the deep effects of this hammering: because poets in the theatre seem to have failed us, seem to have been incapable of welding together unwavering themes, strong dramatic stories, and beautiful language—to create, in other words, a place where we may discover the larger echoes of ourselves—we begin to suspect that maybe the echoes don't really exist. This seems to me to be the real crisis of the poetic theatre. If the theatre can find no consistently eloquent voice, do we dare speak aloud ourselves?

It all sounds grim, but it really isn't. For three reasons. If we can trust history at all, we discover that each period of poetic renewal in the theatre has been preceded by a period of moral reexamination. The Greek poetic dramatists were nurtured on religious mysteries that tried to clarify man's precarious relationship to his gods. Shakespeare followed a prolonged diet of the Miracle and Morality plays that belabored, as the majority of playwrights are belaboring today, the multitude of goods and evils in the world and what man ought to do about them. The dark poetry of Garcia Lorca was the end product of centuries of sacred, didactic playlets that tried to prescribe the paths of righteousness. We seem to be in something like that "preceding period" right now. Serious playwrights are absorbed in a search for durable values that can be lived with *now,* that can—and must—be reexamined and reclassified. In so doing, they are building up interest for the future. Prose is a fine instrument for classifying values. But only poetry can explain and preserve them. It's a matter of time.

The second reason is that a play is a poem. Automatically. No matter how mundanely prosaic it turns out to be, we mustn't totally despair. If only a modest amount of craft is at work, it fulfills the basic requirements of poetry: it is a selective, compressed, highly distilled series of living images that seeks to transpose life into a higher key; its language is controlled; its movement rhythmic; its ideas are vivid; its impact emotional; its intonations melodic; its objective simple: to give man back a better image of himself than he thought possible; than he could have made himself. So while we're waiting for the period of moralizing to end, for the poets to be convinced they can perform the welding they were put on this planet to do, it's some comfort to know that both in its conception and in its nature, a play is already a poetic design.

There is, thirdly, somewhat greater comfort in recalling that man himself is a poetic metaphor. If he isn't, a great deal of ink and blood have been wasted trying to probe his uniqueness and complexity, the strange amalgam of desires in which he seems to embody the desires of all men. If this is the case, you and I—by virtue of trying to contain within this physical shell (the Form) the multitude of ideas and feelings (the Content), and by measuring out the days and hours of our actions (the Meter) in order to realize certain personal objectives (the Stanzas) in the hope of finding some sort of ultimate satisfaction (the Theme)—have no reason to be timid in the face of a poem. We've been writing one for years.

And when everyone believes it, the professional poets will be ready to take over.

iv

Heroes, Non-Heroes, Anti-Heroes

Try to imagine, if you will, that a formal debate is in progress. On the one side is Horatio Alger; on the other Walter
Mitty. The proposition to which they are both addressing
themselves is: Be it resolved that man has a future. Assuming we can overcome our squeamishness about such a subject, its faintly laughable nature, and pay close attention to
the respective arguments of the two debaters, we might
expect to hear a lively clash of ideas. Their positions seem
clear enough: Alger takes the affirmative position that there
is still room for individual heroism, for the head-on collision course with nature, for the insistence that the man
shape the world; Mitty takes the negative, advocating flight
into the dream, acquiescing to ready-made images of glory
that can be achieved by merely throwing the eyes out of
focus. On the surface, at least, the lines of argument seem
sharply drawn. (In actual fact, Mitty isn't listening very
hard to his opponent's reasoning; he's standing there dreaming of *being* the opponent.) In truth, however, there's virtually nothing separating them. Both agree that man has a
future; but Alger sees it as a viable *deed,* Mitty as a vagrant
dream. Alger acts; Mitty adjusts. Alger moves outward and
stands alone; Mitty drifts inward and cherishes his ano-
nymity. Alger paces; Mitty tiptoes. This hypothetical debate

resolves nothing, of course. Both men share too strong a romantic disposition to be completely hostile to one another; both are fundamentally dreamers, and thus a little unrealistic. Both wish to conquer *something*.

As pointless as the debate may seem, and as accurately as we may predict the respective arguments, the question continues to be pressed: is the climate of 20th-century life conducive to the existence of the heroic man? If so, what kind of heroism are we talking about? What kind of man?

Obviously, such questions have infinite theological, sociological, and moral overtones. So abundant, in fact, that they represent the great lump in civilization's throat. No one has found the solution that will wash it down. But while learned men are searching for clues, the theatre is suffering the greatest consequences and paying the heaviest penalties.

The theatre is rather like a tuning fork: it can give off nothing until it is struck by a significant human force. If the blow is heavy or light, precisely placed or bungled, the quality of the tone is bound to be affected. The size, shape, and duration of vibrations the theatre can generate are in direct proportion to the value and weight of the human act that energizes them. Thus, the impact of any hero-concept is bound to have both a theoretical and practical effect on the impact of the theatre on its own society. Big hero: big theatre; little hero: little theatre.

The fact is that for nearly two thousand years the concept of a hero—of that creature who sees and knows himself wholly enough to direct his own destiny and shape the universe into *his* image—has endured the most unimaginably relentless battering. Does the rough definition of "hero" just offered offend you? Does it amuse? Does it strike you as impossibly naïve? It should. It is offensive, amusing, and naïve. It's the sort of definition appropriate to a cloistered university seminar, or made in the fashion of offering one's girl friend the moon and the stars.

There's more at stake, however, in the demoralization of the hero-image than meets the skeptical eye. The loss can't simply be brushed away, like a nagging mosquito, or swatted with such contemptuously innocent remarks such as "Oh, well, we've changed a lot," or "What do you expect from an era of mass, standardized culture?" or "Life's too complicated. It's better to stay out of trouble," or "Well, committees do all the deciding now." Please understand: I'm not myself contemptuous of such remarks; I'm not sermonizing for the sake of filling the reader with guilt because he dropped the ball. I'm quite sure I've made these remarks myself.

So why persist? Why do we continue to feel the loss of heroes and heroics so keenly, so nostalgically? The reason is not really very complicated. Remember: a civilization or a culture makes—or unmakes—its own heroes. The temper and durability of hero-images are a form of judgment the civilization passes on itself. Where these images are weak, or simply don't exist, the stature of all men declines, forcing them to run for shelter and self-importance into manufactured *groups*—whether social, political, religious, or economic. In a market where the hero jobs are either closed or gone begging, the expert, the genius, the boat-rocker is a freak. And not wanting as a rule, to raise our children, or ourselves, as freaks, we moderate a number of absolute standards and goals, taking comfort in the fact that the perils of adaptation to an existing climate are hard enough. In short, we are again passing judgment on ourselves.

Well, we know all this is disturbing, and we all attempt to combat the problem in our special ways. For the theatre, however, this disturbance has taken the form of what theatre historian and critic George Kernodle once labeled the "little man." He's the creature who has absorbed into himself—in a way strangely reminiscent of the suffering Christ-figure— many of the features that used to be more equitably distributed. That is to say: he is something of a hero (or nurses along a few old dreams of being one) but is at the same time his own worst enemy; he is invariably oppressed (as a good protagonist should be), but he is often his own oppressor. In short, he is the deity who creates the demon in his own image. What makes him "little," we can guess, is that the weight of both roles is perhaps too much for him. He shrinks under them rather than, as we might hope, discovering that perhaps now, at last, he has a more complete reckoning of his own resources; and now being both St. George *and* the dragon, his power has been doubled, not diminished.

But he doesn't see it that way, as a rule; certainly playwrights haven't seen it that way. Indeed, they see a man, really quite ordinary in most respects, reasonably faithful to a handful of modest ideals (wife, family, the business index, and a sort-of-God), unaware of what might be profound implications of his thoughts and actions, an incipient humanist sailing with a moderately reliable compass; often victimized, plagued with disquieting ambitions that he cannot accurately name or satisfactorily fulfill, subjected to and quite helpless against the demands of social conventions and restraints; getting along, controlling his dreams just this side of sanity.

Such a generalized portrait risks being inaccurate. But it's familiar and widespread enough to persuade most of the major playwrights of the past fifty years to install this figure as something of the suffering saint of the contemporary stage.

Mr. Kernodle, writing in the *Carleton Drama Bulletin*, describes him a bit more vividly:

> For three decades now modern drama has tried to find a new dream for a city man—a new vision of the importance of life in a mass culture. The old dreams we brought with us from the farms, the grandmothers, the

small towns, the frontiers, the river boats, the gold mines, the duck hunts, have very little to do with the way we actually live today. Never in history has there been such a difference in the way men dream and the way they live. The old dreams were of great individuals, working alone, exploring alone, fighting alone. Today we work in factories, in offices, in teams. Willy Loman dreams of Uncle Ben going into the jungle alone and coming out rich. But today's prospector is a whole team of geologists and engineers. It's been twenty-five years since Lindbergh flew the Atlantic— the last lone hero we have had. Today we fly in teams, with a well-organized ground-crew to keep us going. We live in apartments or in rows of suburban houses. Yet our old dreams tell us we are not a success unless we build a big white house on a hill. We make music in choirs and orchestras, but our novels and movies still show us the great lone individual. Modern life is torn between the outer life of one way of living and the inner life of a different way of dreaming. We try to find a new self, but we feel lost in the vast impersonality of a big city. Can you imagine King Arthur wrangling patiently with a labor committee? Can you see Columbus sitting still on a streetcar or bus? Would Daniel Boone wait in a cafeteria line? Would Tom Edison punch a clock or Andrew Carnegie wait for the Christmas bonus or the Union raise? No! None of our old heroes would have known how to live in a modern city.

We might append to that: neither do our new heroes.

Mr. Kernodle raises some mournful shadows: the old planting, spinning, and handcrafting occupations that ostensibly gave man a peculiar integrity—as the current "do-it-yourself" fascination tries to propagate—and a spiritual unity with Nature that helped him to fathom his own impact upon her. Such integrity and unity made matters like the hope for a God and the promise of man's own durability seem altogether feasible; enough in fact, to inspire the kinds of myths that could serve as yardsticks for heroes. Kernodle then puts a finger on the wrenching shift from agrarian to urban cultures, the attendant loss of self-utility, and the consequent undermining of a few of the key props of hero-hood. (It's interesting, if a little unpleasant, to acknowledge how the mass media—notably television—is so much better attuned to some of the deeper myths and memories than we often give the medium credit for. Many of the least desirable TV programs—The Green Acres, Beverly Hillbillies, nearly all the Westerns, the Gomer Pyles, the Andy Griffiths, the Petticoat Junctions (there are too many to ignore the trend) —all perpetuate the wonderous myth of man back in rhythm with nature, of dealing with it in serenely uncomplicated terms. Remember Willy Loman's last positive act on earth? Cultivating his postage-stamp garden? So more than the avaricious businessmen out in Television City are affected.)

Yet Kernodle's argument is really only part of the explanation for the fall of the hero. And it's a part that modern playwrights have not wholeheartedly accepted. Rice, Anderson, Behrman, Miller, Inge, and Williams have argued, through the instrument of their plays mostly, that if modern man is out of tune with universal melodies and has lost his tragic or heroic stature, there is still ample opportunity for tragic-like and heroic-like actions in his more humble efforts to coexist with his forlorn ambitions. (A cunning answer, to be sure. Being a little frail and forlorn ourselves at times, we are relatively easy marks for anyone who says that we are still—somehow—worthy of recognition.)

And where support for the middle-class hero seems uncertain, the playwrights have argued that to beat the drums for membership in the S.P.G.T.H. (Society for the Preservation of Greek Tragic Heroes) is preposterous. We aren't Greeks; we aren't ancient; and social, scientific, and religious institutions are equipped to absorb the "thousand natural shocks" that a hero was heir to.

Some playwrights, most notably O'Neill, have tried to persuade us that the whole matter was totally anemic and academic; erased from our consciousness. But he couldn't quite sell that argument, least of all to himself.

So the rationales for not having, or not needing, hero-images multiply and divide and multiply again, maneuvering us—whether we like it or not—into a conglomerate of philosophies and speculations that have become virtually clichés of modern life. Before they become entirely clichés, it's worthwhile to retrace a little of the evolution of the 20th-century "little man" and try to indicate how he got so small.

Since about 1920, Kernodle reminds us that there have been three distinct reactions to, or ways of dealing with, the image of the small guy who has been trapped by an incomprehensible maze of routines and ambitions that have gradually eroded him.

The 1920's tried to laugh him away and produced, as a consequence, the *funny* little man, the helpless cog in the big machine, the cipher, so tightly spun into his own cocoon of failure that he lost his resilience as a human being and became almost like a wind-up toy, clicking and whirring toward disaster without half realizing it. It's the old Bergsonian idea that when a man loses his capacity to respond, when he remains rigid in the face of change, he becomes an object of laughter. So we laughed at Mr. Zero in the *Adding Machine,* we screamed over Charlie Chaplin in *City Lights* or *Modern Times* (and still do), we roared at Harold Lloyd, even as he blundered into one outrageously pathetic misadventure after another.

By the 1930's society was being shaken by economic disorders at home and by threatening political manipulations abroad. The little man wasn't funny any more. He wanted to fight back, to treat violence with violence. In life, the archtype was Adolph Hitler, who set out to punish the world to satisfy his personal grievances and maladjustments. And in becoming a fighter, he turned into a virtual ape-man. Remember Tommy Turner in *The Male Animal:* a mild, easily humiliated college professor at the beginning, a roaring beast of the new jungle at the end, ready to beat off the predators and, if necessary, drag his woman back to the cave by her hair. Clifford Odets was especially skillful in creating images of the ape-man. The Golden Boy himself, from an insignificant lower class background, clinging to vague dreams of being a musician, but finally having to use his fists to win any sort of recognition. The motion pictures, of course, were crammed with ape-men who were usually victims of one kind of social malaise or another, turning finally to the gun, to the bottle, to the streets in order to win back, if a little perversely, some of the honor they have been denied. O'Neill, even earlier, put hair on his ape. And Lennie, in *Of Mice and Men,* so completely a product of the forest, even betrays his own kind, another little man.

The 1940's tried to dream the little man away, and by escaping into the nest of illusion tried to rediscover some new significance, a more tenable relationship between the real and the mythical worlds. For nearly two decades the dream syndrome hung on—until, later, it was to turn into a nightmare. Examples of the syndrome are legion: Elwood Dowd dreams of Harvey, the rabbit, as a source of friendship; Anita Loos dreams of phosphorescent barrooms and the security it offers in *Happy Birthday;* Saroyan spins the dream of a home, in *My Heart's in the Highlands,* and of purity, that house on the hill, the sleeping dog, in *The Time of Your Life.* ("What's the dream, Kitty Duval?" Joe asks the prostitute. And, of course, she has one—in wide screen and technicolor.)

Nearly every major character in the rich dramatic file of Tennessee Williams' plays lives fiercely in this world expressly for the purpose of dreaming of another. *The Glass Menagerie,* surely one of his best, is a gallery of dreams: Amanda has a vision of Southern gentility that was probably never hers; Laura is possessed by an idealized and fragile dream of romance—as fragile as her glass animals; Tom, of being a poet and finally freeing himself of having to live with illusion ("Blow out your candles, Laura," he pleads at the end of the play). When Blanche DuBois, the neurotic, dream-infested girl encounters Stanley, the orthodox ape-man, there is trouble. Many of the dreams that obsess Williams' heroines are not especially pleasant; in fact, they're more like festering things that spread throughout the organism and gradually weaken the entire mind and body.

And still the dream syndrome persists. What, after all, is Willy Loman's problem but a vision of success, of paternal responsibility, of domestic tranquillity that will not be realized, even though he keeps materializing Uncle Ben as a means of reassuring himself that Horatio Alger is stronger than Walter Mitty. Yet when all's done, Charley is obliged to announce that "a salesman's got to dream, boy. It comes with the territory."

Apparently, this applies to more than salesmen. If playwrights have been reading the signs correctly, we seem to be spending most of our time unplugged from the real world, happily disconnected from the current of actuality that sweeps around and through us. So obligatory has become the use of dream, of memory, or of nostalgia as devices to expose character and express conflict in a play that the invocation of a dream, of the recollection of some wholly past experience or desire, has become a major technique of play construction. This is, at best, a questionable approach to playwrighting because it seems to violate what was, once, considered a fundamental tenet of the theatre; that is, that all action on the stage reinforce the forward motion of the play. Indeed, the most desirable dramatic quality the writer was once obliged to create was the incessant, onward-moving, unimpeded thrust of the action. It was one of the special gifts and special delights that the theatre could provide. Now, however, we must repeatedly tether our emotions while a character pours himself a drink, wanders to the window, gets the peculiarly dilated look in his eyes, and starts unwinding a piece of reminiscence that often begins: "It didn't always used to be this way. Remember the first time you walked into my laboratory, when I was injecting the hormones into my pet panther. You laughed. You always laughed when you looked at my panther. Or was it at my serum? You rushed over to me," etc.

To be sure, there is a valid need for such reminiscing. It gives a sense of history and perspective to the characters and story, it serves often to motivate subsequent actions, it can even serve, occasionally, as a decisive turning point in the life of a dramatic figure. What I'm referring to is the massive, total substitution of reflection for action and the awful inertia that begins to infest the play when it happens. You get a sense of such frustration, such futility, such deadening lack of movement that the impulse is to scream: or, more discreetly, to get up and leave the theatre. Where Cyrano found something to *do* (and that's the critical verb of the theatre), George (in *Virginia Woolf*) finds something to *say,* and usually in the form of some bitter recollection, some vindictive insult he gleefully dredges up from the past.

So the dream-obsessed little man of the last two and one-half decades has had a very large effect on the art of dramaturgy. Not a particularly wholesome effect. Playwrights seem to have lost, or at least have mistakenly fore-sworn, the skill of structuring their dramas as a progressive, steadily intensifying, and climactic series of human *actions* —actions that would both propel the play forward and serve as legitimate catalysts for dreams. They have been forced, like either Williams or Inge, into often ugly and disfigured memories as a means of holding attention; or like Miller, into pseudoexpressionistic chronicle histories (*After the Fall* —a triumph of *retrogressive* action); or like the Absurdists who sensibly ridicule the whole inert mess, as Ionesco ridi-culed it in, say, *The Bald Soprano* or Albee in *The Ameri-can Dream*. (As you may gather, some of the most exciting drama in the 20th-century theatre has not occurred as dramatic stories; rather, it's taken the form of aesthetic in-fighting, the scorn and rupturing of one theatrical form in favor of another.)

This sense of inertia that seems to characterize the affairs of the little man begins to explain, in part, why certain rather trivial and transient pieces became so dispropor-tionately popular: *The Solid Gold Cadillac, No Time for Sergeants, At War with the Army,* and the recent revival of *You Can't Take It with You*. These were all plays in which dreams came true, in which the impersonal force (big business, the military, the Internal Revenue Service) were outsmarted by the little guy. But note the irony involved: when the little man triumphs, the play is usually treated as comedy, or even farce. It's almost as if the playwright were saying that no one would take him seriously any other way.

So we live in the precinct of the little man, or what we may now call by his more official title: the non-hero. The metamorphosis of the hero into the non-hero, as I've already suggested, has been going on for a long time. Clear back to those resolute skeptics of Ancient Greece, Aristophanes and Euripides, both of whom described the clay-footed nature of the gods and other legendary figures. The sacrosanct

Athenian society finally had to squelch Aristophanes for having gods lowered in a basket, for showing mighty titans wrapped up against the chill and protected by umbrellas, and for depicting businessmen as sinister, exploiting villains. Euripides tried to humanize his characters; he married Electra off to a shepherd and later declared, through the mouth of the old grandmother in *The Trojan Women,* the universal heartbreak of an irrational and violent act that an ordinary mortal was powerless to control.

But the most formidable and persistent instrument for the decline of the hero was the entire Hebraic-Christian myth, that resynthesis of a hundred unquenchable beliefs and rituals that span back to Bacchus, back to Osiris in Egypt, back to totemic tribes, back into the folk legends of nameless cults, all of which struggled to find a way to explain and to assimilate unidentifiable forces into their daily experiences.

No matter how it is viewed, no matter how reverently or discreetly treated, the Hebrew-Christian tradition developed, through the conscious will of man, into a conscious system that subordinated man. His knowledge, his will, and his destiny became subject to the omniscient authority of a single God. When the Lord became our Shepherd, our trip through life became a guided tour. Grace, repentance, good works, and salvation provided the loopholes in life's contract. A model was needed: a working, earthly model to demonstrate the kind of humility, compassion, and suffering that all men should emulate. Christ, of course, was such a model; put on earth as a willing receptacle for the sins and errors of mankind, and going to his death as a gesture of both love and obedience.

It's a rich tradition, to be sure; indeed, especially rich if we are willing to give some credit for it not only to divine revelation but also to the persisting humanist tradition so basic to the careful construction of such a tradition.

But it's not the tradition itself that's of concern here; we'll allow the professional skeptics and the avowed believers to thrash it out. What *is* of concern is the irreparably altering effect of this tradition on the image of man and its subsequent translations onto the stage. Heroism lost its autonomy, its reference to only its own designs. It was hard, if not impossible, to construct a macrocosm—a greater universe—solely out of the pieces intrinsic to man himself. Deference, submission, and reluctance became greater hallmarks of life than defiance.

A genuine act of heroism requires a high degree of calculated blindness to all prevailing dogma and codes. It's not a matter of merely being defiant toward God, or toward social institutions, or toward other people. Such defiance is often transient in nature, usually resulting in noisy social protest that has only limited objectives. The kind of heroic defiance that I'm suggesting has been foresworn as a result of a continuing preoccupation with the Hebraic-Christian ethic is an act that draws its power, sometimes arrogantly it seems, from the capacity of one man to live alone—a *free* man—unintimidated by conventions or mysteries, unobsessed by prejudices or creeping frailties, unthreatened by the threats of the holy or the seductions of the impious. Such freedom is rare; and like anything rare, it represents a dream, the myth of the kind of primal serenity and satisfaction that most human beings may only covet. This myth is the keystone in the arch of the hero. Without it, the stones loosen and tumble.

The Enlightenment also contributed to the fall of the arch. Ironical, too. For nearly a century and a half the celebration of man's prowess as a reasoning creature went on; nature was getting less hostile; the universe was beginning to seem containable in the pyramidal cells of the brain; logic was enshrined as a source of man's ultimate authority over beasts. And some of the newer notions that evolved from all the studies restored some respectability to the ideas of freedom, democracy, and equality; dignified them just enough, in fact, to make us suddenly realize that the egalitarian underpinning of these ideas was the anathema to the ideas of heroes and heroism. Where all things are equal, the hero —who is, after all, an unequally dimensioned creature—is an anachronism. Where cultural and political strata are obliterated—at least ideologically—how can we measure the number of strata a hero has penetrated? The right to defy as well as the obligation to obey was, theoretically, *everyone's* privilege, distributed liberally even among those who could not, by any stretch of the imagination, be considered equipped to be free.

If you are beginning to detect something fundamentally imperious and austere about the nature of heroism, you detect rightly. Trained in the familiarities of a paternalistic democracy and religious experience, our view of the potential of a hero is bound to breed a little contempt—or at least confusion.

The tottering hero-image received three final shoves early in the 20th century, Kernodle reminds us. The first of the three events was simple enough: the publication of Spengler's *Decline of the West.* The book attempted to prove that modern man had moved into an urban mass of colorless, standardized ciphers—the Mr. Zeros of *The Adding Machine,* the Dr. Rices in *Beggars on Horseback,* even the Supreme Court Justices in *Of Thee I Sing.* Spengler contended that it was no longer possible for an individual to create anything original or significant. In general, his arguments were most persuasive, even though subsequent developments and historians have perforated Mr. Spengler. But as an interim crystallization of a continuing condition, it had more than its share of influence in convincing us that we were even more rapidly becoming helpless blobs.

The second event was the defeat of Germany in 1918.

This last great war, like the defeat of the Spanish Armada, should have bolstered our spirits, proving us right, invincible. It didn't, of course. We weren't too enthusiastic about going into it in the first place. ("I Didn't Raise My Boy To Be a Soldier" was a hit song of the popular stage.) And we very shortly discovered what a particularly dirty and dishonorable war it was, how it demolished the final traces of dignity and gentlemanliness and erased all lingering memories of plumed steel helmets, tidy battlelines of stamping steeds, and codes of honor. And Germany was defeated, not by heroic individuals, but by inundating battlefields with hundreds of thousands of men—numbered, tagged, virtually faceless and nameless men—spilling out over trenches. Oh, the Sergeant Yorks appeared now and then; we couldn't let all those medals go to waste. But the final, triumphant figure to emerge from the war was this numbered, tagged, faceless, nameless, sublimely *anonymous* image of the *unknown* soldier. Having accepted and enshrined a symbol as a substitute for a person, it was easier still to believe that the insularity we had cherished as a nation, which was furthermore an ingredient of heroism, had to be totally abandoned.

The third event was in the nature of a shocking discovery. For the first time in national history, army induction centers of World War I conducted intelligence tests on a mass scale. Out of all the testing came the frightening little figure of the moron. The horrifying spectacle of great lumps of Americans demonstrating that they had the mental age of thirteen took a while to absorb. Psychologists tried to explain how inaccurate was the popular interpretation of the test results —as they still do today with I.Q. tests—but the myth persisted. Jokes, stories, films, plays, and new character types became dedicated to the moron or variations thereof, most commonly the addle-pated bungler (usually a husband or father) who bumbled through a thousand situation comedies in films, radio, and television. Even today, Jerry Lewis continues the tradition of the moron in his films, sentimentalizing the type, naturally, but a boob nonetheless.

It's no wonder that the conniving gods on Madison Avenue seem to be content with this World War I estimate of the American population; except that Madison Avenue is more conservative: they drop the mental age to twelve.

Protected by the walls of our own cerebral security and worldly sophistications, it may be difficult to accept these three events as personally very meaningful. As yardsticks of our own intuitions and actions, they may, indeed, mean nothing. But they did occur; they do represent a continuation of the downward drift of the hero-image; they have been used by subtler minds than ours to underscore a number of deadly gaps in the functioning of a democratic civilization and in the national—and largely disquieting—American character. Above all, the decline of the hero *is* the implicit theme adopted by all the major playwrights of the contemporary realistic theatre. Our finest theatrical talents remain absorbed by this theme and by the image of the non-hero.

Fortunately, the image is being used to good, if temporary, advantage. Tennessee Williams tends to place the non-hero in a psychiatric, guilt-ridden clinic; Miller in a socio-economic, also guilt-ridden, clinic; Inge in the same clinic, but in a much smaller room; Simon in a romanticized, domestic setting; Albee puts him in a torture chamber, in which the most frightening instrument is the man himself.

One of the dangers in the manipulation of this non-hero, which is another way of accepting the deterministic view of human nature (i.e., events make the man), is that sooner or later, critic Robert Corrigan observed (*Forum,* Summer, 1959), the playwright will fail to distinguish between the hero and the victim, between Destiny and Society. Corrigan went on to say:

The consequence in the 20th century has been a theatre of steadily diminishing stature. This is related to
yet another result of the problem of "modernism"
which has had even more profound effects on the
drama. . . . Let us watch our playwright in the process
of creation. He cannot help but have absorbed a great
deal that psychology has made known. He knows all
about the relationship of infantile frustration and adult
neuroses; he has learned about the psychosomatic aspects of illness; and above all he knows that all human
actions—even the greatest and most selfless of them—
spring from some deep and hidden but nonetheless
selfish motivation. Doesn't he feel that there is a danger
in passing a moral judgment on individuals? In fact,
how can there be a moral pattern to human experience
in such a world? For example: a man may commit a
murder; but wait, we know that he saw something
horrible in the barn when he was a child; we discover
that he was brought up on the lower East Side without
orange juice and cod liver oil, and that his mother was
a whore. How can we blame him for this murder that
he was eventually driven to commit? Yes, we can put
him in jail or an asylum; we can even take his life. But
this is because he is dangerous to society and does not
necessarily invoke moral condemnation. If, then, our
moral judgments can be dissolved by psychological understanding, how can the dramatist pattern a tragedy
or create characters with stature? If there is no possibility for an appraisal of personality as such, why
should Hamlet's death be any more significant than
that of Rosencrantz or Guildenstern?

Why, indeed? Mr. Corrigan puts a sharp finger on the
pivotal crisis facing the modern playwright, a crisis that is
both moral (as he indicates) and aesthetic. When the

agonies of the non-hero, the little man, the helpless *nebbish* that seems to lurk in all our skins are explained away by predetermined and incontestable influences on his life, much of his dramatic impact and singularity are drained away. As our subconscious sympathies are activated by clutching at the wisps of run-over dogs, drunken fathers, or even obscure prenatal influences, it drastically diminishes our response to the uniqueness and individual destiny of the creature who is physically there before us on the stage.

Recollect, if you will, how many minutes you have spent in the theatre contemplating the hero's *past* rather than his present, how you've been stirred by his sexual aberration of twenty years before rather than his dynamic struggle to overcome the memory now. Consider one of Albee's finer plays, *The Zoo Story*. If you watch and listen carefully, you will observe two specimens impaled on deterministic lances; and you will come away from a performance deeply imbued by parakeets, lecherous landladies, dogs who won't die, and various other accessories of society that stultify human relations. For all the bravura acting possibilities of the piece, both Peter and Jerry remain utterly *inert* characters, rather like resonating chambers in which assorted moral diseases are amplified.

Is this deterministic philosophy, then, with its inadequate spokesman, the little man, so firmly entrenched as to eliminate any hope for stature or tragic dimensions? Certainly not. There are moral and ethical crises as profound as any an eager, ancient Greek might think up. Trying to live serenely and completely in a world we are threatening to disintegrate is a pretty good crisis for starters. The continuing threat to personal integrity and creativity by the inevitable static forces of the Establishment is fine for a followup. (We can recall the crucifying of J. Robert Oppenheimer, whose sins of the past—i.e., Communist leanings—like avenging Fate, swept in from behind, spurred on by witch-hunters who were themselves deeply vulnerable, nearly caused the professional destruction of one of the formidable scientific minds of the century. A fine germinal idea for a contemporary tragedy: a man with the knowledge, will, and frailties—all in heroic proportions—being forced to come to terms with a timid, non-heroic age.)

The search for stature may be academic and even a little wistful. What makes it so is the apparent malleability of current attitudes, the unusually high boiling point we seem to enjoy, which permits us to endure remarkably intense social heat without popping our lids. We seem to be tolerant in a peculiar way, thanks mostly to psychological and spiritual insights and directives, most of which are used to excuse ourselves from active encounters with life. Thus, we can only be stunned, or perhaps numbed, by an action or an event that develops with tragic decision and swiftness, that leaves us adrift with no tangible or apparent motives other than the relatively lame and inexplicable one: "the man willed it so." More than likely, we share the reaction of the old father in Hebbel's *Maria Magdalena,* who can find no way of dealing with the multitude of disappointments and disasters in his family other than in the pathetic final words of the play: "I don't understand it." The hero knows. The non-hero never finds out. The hero knows because he already enjoys a working kinship with the gods he is destined to aggravate. The non-hero doesn't know because he can no longer identify the gods.

Unfortunately, before these remarks can be complete, we must take one step further down the hero ladder. While the hero felt equal to his world, and the non-hero felt usurped by it, our final category—the anti-hero—is virtually left out of it altogether. How did he come into existence?

In truth, he's been evolving for some time. Having surrendered the old dream of a stable universe, of a society comfortably wrapped up in itself—the kind of society that could build reasonably firm premises for heroes to stand on —we've accepted instead a totally unstable universe that persists in raising annoying questions about everything from the meaning of personal desires to the theories about the origin of the solar system. Once Freud, Darwin, and Marx challenged the facts and necessities of existence, and philosophers such as Schopenhauer and Bergson ostensibly illustrated the shifting realities of existence, it was inevitable that artists of the theatre should express their own special adaptations to strong social ideas.

In his play, *Les Victimes du Devoir,* Ionesco has a character say:

> Inspiring me with a different logic and a different psychology, I should introduce contradiction where there is no contradiction, and no contradiction where there is what common-sense usually calls contradiction. . . . We'll get rid of the principle of identity and unity of character and let movement and dynamic psychology take its place. . . . We are not ourselves. . . . Personality doesn't exist. Within us there are only forces that are either contradictory or not contradictory.

To put it most simply: we don't exist. We have been shunted, like a train, off the main track; encouraged to sit at a siding; replaced by the glaring contradictions which, presumably, we can no longer live with. There's a powerful conscience at work among those who do the shunting. Rather like a cousin of mine, an eye surgeon, who once announced that he wished he could sever his patient's head from his body in order to study the phenomenon of seeing clinically, dispassionately, without the pestering preoccupations of the patient's pain or personality. So much more could be accomplished, my cousin argued, if only, for just a brief period, the human element could be wiped out completely. Not given to homicide, my cousin hasn't achieved his objective. Nor is he a follower of those who prophesy alienation or noncommunication. But he does express in his own way what Ionesco expressed in *his:* to deal with the ultimate despair of men, we must eliminate man in order to study closely the construction of the despair. And in view of what seems to be one of the primary fascinations of modern philosophers and theologians—the persistent fear of annihilation—it seems fair enough to explore the anatomy of the fear as a means of living with it, even if the carrier of the fear—man—has to be temporarily ignored. There is, indeed, something of the impersonality of science in all this, a point of view at work very similar to the depersonalizing that takes place as census figures are collected or a sociologist sets up a study of, say, intergroup dynamics of middle-income families in South Boston, or the way a geneticist plans both control and random experiences in conducting an experiment.

So the devolution to the anti-hero is not, finally, a source of even deeper frustration or a reason for lustier breast-beating, even though the characteristics of the anti-hero are, generally, unnerving enough. The anti-hero, as Esther Jackson (and others) have so vividly described him, is a man struggling to reconcile a profound inner division. The classical hero, if we understand Aristotle correctly, was a coherent and unified body of specific qualities. He possessed enough knowledge to control his reason, even when he found himself in that perilous spot of vacillating between what his knowledge was telling him is right, and what his *will* was compelling him to do. But above all, he was *conscious* of being pulled from two sides; and it was this consciousness of one's *precise* position on the spectrum of possibilities, and on the fringe of disaster, that could create an Oedipus, an Antigone, a Creon.

Now at the other end of the scale, the anti-hero is a product on an attack on all meaning, on all knowledge (remember the Professor in Ionesco's *The Lesson*), all tradition, and finally on the state of *conscious knowing* itself. The result: philosophic and social shambles; intellectual disunity; emotional incoherence. The man who can say, "I know who I am. I am conscious of my existence and my destiny," is either a curio or a fool. But if he says "I'm not sure. . . . I don't know. . . . What difference does it make?" he has divested himself of most normal human involvements and we feel more comfortable in his presence.

Do you recall the Rajah and the Wise Men episode from Sandburg's "The People, Yes"? The Rajah orders his wise men into confinement so that they may ponder the secrets of life and find its ultimate answer. And the Wise Men confabulate late into the night and return with an answer: born, troubled, died. This doesn't satisfy the Rajah, and he sends them into meditation again. When they finally emerge, they bring the ruler the nearest thing to a finite conclusion. One word: maybe. "Maybe" is a key prop in the construction of the anti-hero. He is, as T. S. Eliot once suggested, merely a projection of many courses of possible action because both his knowledge and his will are riddled with contradictions. He is, in other words, an "unbeing," a transparent void through which the terrible imperatives of life pass freely and unmolested. He is the one thousand piece puzzle with pieces that cannot, or refuse to, interlock. (I don't think it's really significant, but it's amusing to note that jigsaw puzzle manufacturers have come up with the perfect anti-hero puzzle: a blank disc, chopped up into hundreds of weakly defined pieces that torment even the most dedicated puzzle-assemblers. When, and if, it's ever assembled, you have the pleasure of staring at a blank disc, chopped up into hundreds of weakly defined pieces.)

A classic symptom of the anti-hero, and one with the most tantalizing overtones, is the issue of guilt. The anti-hero, we are informed, is guilt-ridden. Well, that's nothing new. Oedipus was guilty, so was Lear, so was Harpagon (in Molière's *The Miser*). The difference, however, lay in how the guilt was acquired. The classical hero, when he offended his gods or his society, was guilty—not of sin, but of limited knowledge. When full knowledge was achieved, he could then weigh the dimensions of his crime, and face whatever music was coming to him. The anti-hero is not permitted such satisfactions. To begin with, he cannot precisely name the guilt—there being altogether too much moral flux around him anyway. Even if he could name it, he'd be hard pressed to locate its source with any accuracy. Society, environment, personality—those amorphous, uncontrollable pressures have become primary culprits, we gather, in the spawning of guilty feelings. Because I am privileged, the poor haunt me. Because I am underprivileged, the rich destroy me. Because I was loved, the hatred of the world intimidates me. Because I am weak, the strong take advantage of me. As a consequence of the unnamed guilt and its indefinable source, the anti-hero has become a wanderer, an alien, searching for the means to expiate a guilt he wasn't born with and didn't know he developed; struggling to reconcile his own puzzling, unfixed existence with an even more puzzling cluster of suspicions and contradictions that the world has announced are out to get him.

The most serious upshot of this condition is the effect of alienation, apparently the most grievous form of suffering. Having found no tenable faiths in the outside world, and having been impressed with the prurient, ugly, dispossessed worms that are devouring us from within, we are alienated, both doors are closed, and we remain in a state of physical and moral chaos that is, presumably, characteristic of the state of all men.

Christ might have been an anti-hero. By undertaking, and dying for, sins he did not personally commit, he might be charged by the rationalist with perpetrating the kind of senseless, alienated act that seems to distress 20th-century man. But Christ really doesn't qualify. He had a third door, a third universe entirely that would remain open to him.

Of all the anti-hero's quirks, this matter of alienation is the most lethal. It has become a major perspective in contemporary thought, the source of many sociological hypotheses and of literary visions. Two world wars, a devastating depression, expanding disenchantment with socialism and with much social liberalism, and, perhaps most important, a widening sense of restlessness and frustration amid affluence are everywhere today. Within such an environment, the wars in Korea and South Vietnam are logical probabilities. And with no tenable utopia on the horizon, the fact of alienation, of estrangement from old faiths, of loneliness among multitudes, will continue to seem the essential motif in the lexicon of the artist, especially the theatre artist. Our little friend Tinker Bell, obviously, cannot live in such an environment.

Almost all the principal works of contemporary playwrights reflect the preoccupation with this environment. It's deep in the foundations of nearly every O'Neill play, it's found in *All My Sons, Death of a Salesman* ("Oh, what's the use, Pop. You're a dime a dozen," says the son, expressing the futility, the pointlessness of experience), *After the Fall,* and *Incident at Vichy,* in nearly every Tennessee Williams play, in *Slow Dance on the Killing Ground,* in *The Subject Was Roses,* in *Marat Sade* (boldly carried to its logical extremes), in *The Zoo Story* and in *Virginia Woolf.* In all of them are the dynamic currents of disenchantment and patent culpability, of complicity with the world's evils. The final effect of these plays is mordant, desperate, and despairing. Worse than that, they lie; they commit fashionable lies in order to remain in vogue; they prefer to thrash around in already choppy waters rather than try to swim toward something; they portray the agony in all its splendor without confessing that the agony may be, at least in part, only a temporary disfigurement of a dream. Not a Kitty Duval dream, but a dream of reason, of purpose, of willingness to find an object of trust that might serve as a reliable road sign. They employ artistic forms with the belligerence and redundance of longshoremen, forgetting that even if the message is sour, the form may still be sweet and can offer, through aesthetic design, a redeeming statement about man's prerogatives.

Indeed, I sometimes wonder if American playwrights know *why* both the non-hero and the anti-hero have emerged; I wonder sometimes if they know the essential purpose for using them and dramatizing their problems. I wonder if they know that the anti-hero is the 20th century's Everyman, condemned to wander until he can find and declare a value to his life. And like his medieval counterpart, the anti-hero is a warning, a walking maxim, a moral syllogism ("The world is evil; man lives in the world; therefore, man is evil") that cannot be logically and universally proven. The message of the anti-hero is abundantly clear: get involved. We *know* we're not; certainly not as much as we should be. It seems to me, then, that the function of a meaningful theatre is to show us *how*.

It may not be long before this will happen. The hero, as we have seen, has passed from the image of the imperfect, conscious man to the perfectly unconscious man. Before he can be reinvested with awareness and self-honor, there will have to be a dynamic realignment of those social and moral values that are basic to a tenable hero-concept. Such a realignment is already under way.

For centuries now, two seemingly opposing ideas have been on a collision course. On one track, humanism (the idealization of self-sufficient man); on the other, the Revealed Word (as manifested in various religious beliefs).

The gap between them has been closing with a velocity that can scarcely be described. It's exciting to speculate on the results of this collision, on the prospects of a new amalgam of ideas that may produce new foundations for the spiritual autonomy of men.

Signs of the imminent contact are everywhere, from the ecumenical movement in Rome, to the worker-priests in Marseilles, to the informal coffeehouse congregations in cellars in New York City, to the Off-Broadway theatre run with verve and imagination by Protestant clergymen, to the increasing stature of religious drama on television. Yes, even to the whole "God is Dead" movement which is serving as a potent housecleaning instrument to clarify what values, if any, remain. The two opposing ideas are so dangerously close that it's hard to tell a humanist from a religionist without a program. It has become altogether too common to hear a young clergyman choose as text for his sermon not Isaiah, not the Epistles, but Camus or Sartre.

The promise of this collision, with its probable shaking up and discarding of irrelevant, atrophied parts on both sides, is one of the most encouraging signs in the 20th century. But until it occurs—and it may even take positive shape in our lifetime—we will have to be patient with the theatre, sweat out its parasitic attachment to the futility of existence, and give sympathetic ear to the passionate polemics of the playwrights—the subject of the next chapter—who are struggling to make old myths compatible with new moralities. If the amalgam can be realized, the heroes may emerge. And with them, Tinker Bell.

V

The Modern Medievalists

Have you noticed something strange about the major post-war playwrights? They don't write *plays* anymore. It would almost seem as if the crowning disillusionment that the World War II represented made the writing of plays a distinctly superfluous activity; that is, if you are a *serious* playwright, with an aggravated sense of responsibility and have concluded that—life being what it is—there's nothing playful in a play any more. Treatises and lessons are written (by Brecht), existential exercises are written (by Camus and Sartre), personal testaments and social exposés are written (by Miller), anti-plays are written (by Ionesco), excursions into religious mysticism are written (by Eliot and Betti), and social critiques are written (by Dürrenmatt and Frisch) —but almost no one writes plays. (I think David Belasco was the last one who tried.)

To write a play presupposes two conditions: that Nature offers a coherent body of experience that can be resolved into formal techniques and conventions and that, in applying these techniques and conventions, the *form* of the dramatic composition is considered *as important as* the content. We know already, I think—from personal observations as well as from the major drifts in philosophic speculation— that we have reason to doubt Nature (human and otherwise) and, as an inevitable corollary, we acknowledge the *formless* aspects of art. So the notion of a "play," with all its seductive overtures toward making *craft* an *equal* to idea, is fundamentally incompatible with a deranged universe; and it's especially incompatible with the intention of contemporary authors to reexamine ideas *first* in an effort to restore order.

There's an odd blessing connected with this nonplay syndrome present among modern writers. While avidly recording the moral and social fumbling of man, they are fulfilling that vagrant ideal of the old humanist tradition. Do you remember those happy platitudes that expressed the essence of this tradition: "The proper study of mankind is man"; "Man is the measure of all things"; "At the center of the universe stands . . . ," etc.? It almost seems as if, by default, the humanist ideal (the celebration of man) is coming into full flower at a time when the existential ideal (the despair and dislocation of man) is influencing most of our thinking: indeed, at a time when the humanist tradition, deeply scored by doubts and failures, is more urgently needed than ever. Contemporary playwrights would, I think, accept Alexander Pope's estimate of man as someone who is "darkly wise and rudely great," even at the risk of getting lost in the darkness and being dismayed by the rudeness.

With such a responsibility on their hands, the major playwrights—Thornton Wilder, Tennessee Williams, and Arthur Miller—have had to perform some brazen feats of emotional sculpturing. Knowing that we haven't world enough or time to indulge in the heart-warming truths that may be dug out of individual man or the abundant personality traits of a *particular* character, playwrights have been forced to cut away most of the emotional fat in order to transform the particular man into the universal abstraction. And knowing, further, that such surgery is contrary to the desires and expectations of theatre audiences—who, after all, would rather empathize than think—playwrights have been obliged to borrow theatrical devices and to assume a didactic air in order to break through all the comfortable desires and expectations. And so, with the heat on, the serious playwright has been forced to abandon the writing of plays in favor of turning the stage into a lecture hall, a confessional, a courtroom, hoping that what he is arguing, explaining, or apologizing for will have the same appeal that lovers' woes, foreclosing mortgages, and daring rescues used to have.

Of course, it finally doesn't work that way. Bertolt Brecht struggled honorably to keep the audience at arm's length, to prevent them from enjoying their time-honored right to feel and to identify with the travails of his characters. He even violated logic and memory, intruded on the scene with rasping visual and auditory messages, reduced personality to a strident, single motif, harangued at the audience, waved banners in their faces. But it finally didn't work because audiences have a cunning, atavistic instinct to fill in the blanks, to restore the missing pieces, to reinflate the sterile symbols with as many pounds of emotional association as needed to make them tolerable and understandable. Brecht probably understood the short-term value of denying an audience its pleasures and how it created an aesthetic short-circuit. It probably explains why plays such as *Mother Courage* and *Galileo*—both essentially realistic pieces—will endure while his *Lehrstücke,* the caustic teaching instruments, will become museum pieces.

Brecht, however, is an extreme case. Wilder, Williams, and Miller have never been so bold, have never so completely surrendered to cerebral manipulation of ideas. They have, however, adopted in common two dramatic conventions as media for their arguments: expressionism and allegory. To understand fully what the three playwrights have achieved, and why it has been achieved at considerable cost to themselves and to the human objects they have dramatized, it's essential that the theatrical significance of both expressionism and allegory be reviewed.

As it's most commonly understood, expressionism in the theatre is both a style of production and a philosophical estimate of society. It was developed largely out of the spiritual and economic nightmare that enveloped Germany in the second decade of this century. The national humiliation that followed World War I crystallized the skepticism and despair that had been eroding the political and social foundations of the country for years. Unemployment, hunger, and forced population shifts transformed Nature into a grotesque agent of destruction. This deformed image of reality pervaded all man-made institutions and objects, erasing their sense of permanence and value. Along with objects, human beings lost their humanness, their distinctiveness, and their resilience. The quality of nightmare, of fever dream was everywhere. You need only recall the early silent film, *The Cabinet of Dr. Caligari,* to visualize the threatening tilt of walls, the forbidding and suffocating closeness of streets and alleys, the dehumanized aspect to the characters—who now resemble animated ghosts, bloodless cadavers.

The demoralization of a national culture would have been more than enough inspiration for artists, but there were other pressing issues as well that intensified the atmosphere. The whole issue of class stratification was raised and threatened. With Individual Man having lost his human integrity, the battle for rights and recognition became a class war, and the single hero became the collective hero—the *Masse Mensche* of Ernst Toller's play. The sacrifice was enormous. To win—or even to understand— the battle, personality had to be flattened, ironed out, deliberately blunted. The weight of vast numbers, and the political issue they symbolized, became far more important than the distracting impurities of any one man.

To fuse both the nightmare and the need for political action, playwrights such as Toller, Kaiser, Wedekind, and Hauptmann developed a theatrical shorthand that was stunning in its ferocious emotional impact. Realism (which was unpleasant enough to record) and logic (which didn't seem to obtain any longer anyway) were discarded. Life was treated as an unrelated, disjointed, scattered, and distorted series of encounters that tried to project the inner reality of contemporary experience. With the goal being primarily to express the *essence* of the ordeal, the expressionistic play was built on short, stabbing scenes; dialogue that was terse and telegraphic; characters without individual identity, without history, without future, going by such names as Man, Daughter, Capitalist (and later on the American stage, of course Mr. Zero); and scenic effects that created a visual dissonance. (The American stage was to enjoy a brief but hectic affair with expressionism. Rachel Crothers [*Expressing Willy*], Elmer Rice [*The Adding Machine*], and Kaufman and Connelly [*Beggar on Horseback*] touched the form gingerly and then retreated.)

In its purest form, expressionism was short lived. But its effect was salutary and its influence persistent. It clearly demonstrated that the stage could deal boldly with states of oppression—social, political, or psychological; that drastic departures from realism would draw us closer to the reality of a given situation; that the reduction of character to abstraction was perhaps a much more truthful definition of man in a state of crisis than the "well-rounded" character could ever be—especially when we remember how, in our personal encounters with strong emotional pressure, we are transformed into nearly classic attitudes of, say, grief or joy or pain. In fact, the greater the pressure, the more "self" is surrendered in favor of those postures and manners that relate us to a million other human beings. It's a common enough experience in life; in the theatre, the expressionists molded this experience into images that were both poignant (because of the kinship we feel) and strident (because of the pain endured in sacrificing so much of oneself).

Expressionism, then, as a way of looking at the pivotal crises in life, remains one of the major resources for contemporary playwrights. It's been softened, of course; it's used more subtly, naturally, because even a *very* angry playwright finds it hard to sell his vitriol when we all know that he's being very well fed and very well paid, when his children are enrolled in expensive French-language schools, and when the greatest crisis in his life is to persuade Star X to get along with Director Y. But more importantly, having liberated the stage from its enervating encumbrances, by proving how garrulous and empty the theatre had become, expressionism taught dramatists how to freshly evaluate the old naturalism, to shake some of the redundance out of it, and to come up with a tighter, more vital means of delivering a message. And out of this evaluation, the contemporary playwright found that it was possible to learn a little of what was best from both worlds: from expressionism, a bolder use of symbol and metaphor and a freer handling of time and space; from naturalism, a continuing appreciation for the special characteristics and resonances within the individual character.

At least, this is what Wilder, Williams, and Miller learned, and why all three—at least once in each of their writing careers—turned out a play that paid its respects to the more overt forms of expressionism (*Our Town, Death of a Salesman,* and *Camino Real*).

The second major convention, or resource, that modern serious playwrights have dipped into is one considerably older than expressionism. From the *Odyssey* of Homer, to Dante's nether world, to the sorrowful quest of Everyman, to *Pilgrim's Progress,* to *Peer Gynt,* to *Moby Dick,* we recall that the great literary epics have all been, in a very real sense, allegories, depicting—through the metaphor of the sea, of hell, of foreign climes, and of personal experiences—the image of the wanderer, the man searching for an ultimate answer or for a final confrontation with the forces that have puzzled, awed, or terrified him all his life. And because his search has always been on a grand scale, because his daring has been distinctly superhuman, and because the risks involved are as enormous as the prize, the searcher becomes our personal agent, the embodiment of the dreams we dared not dream alone. The representation of the combat between cosmic and mortal forces has always been a subject for allegorical treatment, primarily as a means of rendering this combat in terms ordinary humans can grasp.

Let me hasten to say that I'm not suggesting that Wilder, Miller, or Williams rank with Homer, Dante, or Melville, or that there is any precise similarity of epic treatment, or that today's ranking playwrights are weaving tomorrow's myths. Not at all. But there has been a natural tendency on the part of these authors to adopt the tradition of the allegory as a means of personifying the combat between the universal and personal forces that exist today. Where the wilderness of the oceans served Homer, the mind of God serves Wilder; where an inferno was a proper setting for Dante, the fire of sexual neuroses satisfies Williams; where a sojourn among the abstract figures of former sins and good deeds became Everyman's ordeal, Miller explores the myths of social institutions that cripple the soul.

We're normally a little reluctant to assign so formidable a designation as "epic" to the affairs of self-destroying, guilty, *little* men. But the affairs *are* epic, nonetheless, for they represent the magnification of the central crises that obsess all men. That figures in modern drama seem to lack the knowledge of being involved in an epic struggle is no reason to scorn the magnitude of that struggle or to unduly demean the figures. If these figures are, indeed, allegorical figures, then it is, presumably, *us* on the stage. And if the characters are unaware of the motives for or consequences of their actions, *we* know. This is the peculiar wrinkle to contemporary allegory: it clarifies the crisis by demanding that we, as an informed, mass audience, become the hero's accomplices and thus, by our collective mass and number, contribute the extra dimension necessary for epic proportions. Willy Loman, by himself, is a pathetic cipher; when he is bolstered by the echoes of Willy that reverberate through many of us, his helpless dream-chasing takes on an alarming magnitude.

So contemporary playwrights, faced with all those well-publicized calamities of modern life, have turned to allegory and expressionism as means of encapsulating the calamities, of reducing them to feasible proportions. But I wonder if these playwrights—and, indeed, if audiences and critics in general—realize what an awkward mixture allegory and expressionism make. Perhaps it is already apparent why the special properties of each make them difficult partners.

Expressionism, remember, is an act of violence, a bald declaration that the world has gone crazy, scattering irrational fragments to the four winds. Conversely, the allegory of man's search is a wholly rational judgment of the world, an assertion that, no matter how much hell there is to pay, no matter how long or hectic the trip, a course is being taken, guided by clear (and, occasionally, mystical) objectives. The allegory, in other words, implies the existence of, as it were, a "home." Expressionism, on the other hand, not only destroys the home but creates a vacuum in its place. This makes, obviously, for aesthetically uneasy bedfellows. But the admixture may not be as strange as it seems.

For one thing, the apparently opposing pulls create a superior form of dramatic tension that you find noticeably lacking in those works (the pop Broadway fare) that adhere to neither tradition. The tension reveals itself, mostly, in the ambivalent nature of the playwright's theme. To put it bluntly, he wants both to have and eat his cake. In the most frenzied dreams of Blanche Dubois, in the most pathetic remembrances of Emily, in the most dreadful exorcisms conducted in Quentin's mind (in *After the Fall*), there is the clinging, parasitic vision of a perfect world, an intact moral order, a destiny that, no matter how aberrant it may seem at the moment, offers fulfillment.

This ambivalence, this two-headed creature that seems to lurk behind so many major dramatic efforts, has roots deep in human endeavors far beyond the theatre. Recently, Professor Smeltzer of the University of California at Berkeley lectured on mass movements. He reminded us that the great hallmark of activist groups—from the advocates of the Townsend Plan in the 1930's to the Neo-Nazi Movement in and around Arlington, Virginia, today—is this very ambivalence: villifying a real or imagined enemy while glorifying a real or imagined destiny. In actual fact, these movements often scorn the very attributes they want for themselves.

This ambivalence is equally true in contemporary drama: impotence is shown, but the dream of virility is barely concealed; despair is dramatized, but the vision of hope is strong. Abuse is piled on abuse until, perhaps, the pile is high enough to reach relief from pain. Dying is not so bad if there's even a vagrant hope of being resurrected. Expressionism takes care of the dying; the allegory of search looks after the resurrection.

How, then, does all this apply to the three playwrights singled out for the present discussion? Pretty well, if we don't get too rigid and deny the authors a fair amount of creative leeway in their own sometimes expressionistic allegory of search for vital new ways to announce old dilemmas.

Thornton Wilder, by almost any measure, is something of a theatrical fluke. He has remained aloof from the militantly sour and scornful attitudes, from the hopeless wallowing in philosophical ambiguities that seem to characterize the 20th century. And by persisting in the veins of love, hope, and charity, he seems rather like a virginal child strolling among deformed lechers. He has not always been treated kindly and thoughtfully because of this; indeed, Wilder's optimistic, chicken-on-Sunday, old-time-religion viewpoint has often irritated those critics who have foresworn church, chicken, and hope. And when they praise at all, it's often by a patronizing reference to "the poet of the commonplace," or by marveling at those clever theatrical shenanigans Wilder cooks up in his plays—recipes that Wilder himself admits are derivative.

In Wilder, then, we see a figure of the forlorn, apparently out-of-tune dramatist who has dedicated his mind and works to the rediscovery of lost, universal melodies, and is in no way intimidated at the prospect of juggling celestial bodies to do it. And out of the rearranging of the spheres comes Wilder's message: that man—brace yourself!—is good; that life is a beautiful and precious commodity, not a fragment of which should be wasted; that even the most simple and commonplace affairs of individual man (the microcosm) are an intrinsic part of a vast cosmic cycle of life (the macrocosm); and that man is not diminished by the awesome prospect of a universal determinism, but rather enriched by it, made a full partner in the grand order of the universe, and ennobled thereby.

Louis Broussard (in *American Drama*) aptly sums up the Wilder philosophy:

> No other writer begins with so hopeful a premise: that this age is essentially no different from any other, that its problems, whatever they may be, since Wilder refuses to give expression to them, will resolve themselves in change which can only be better than the

past. His is not the search for an exit from dilemma; there is no dilemma. If he has advice to give, it is that people continue to love one another.

With such a philosophy, and such a view of time and history, it's easy to understand why a critic such as Mary McCarthy would be offended by a play such as *The Skin of Our Teeth*. She felt that it was a tasteless joke that ignored the shaping and changing force of history, that affirmed the flatness of the present simply because Wilder saw the past as flat too, and that viewed eternity as a happy compendium of capitalist and middle-class values that rigidly resisted change. While there's substantial truth to her arguments, the truth would be stronger still if it were not so deeply colored by her own ideological view of the continuing class struggle and by what was her private version of eternity.

Despite such dyspeptic criticism, Wilder persists in reformulating his allegories on the richness and brevity of life and of man's incomplete passage through it. This is the crux of Wilder's allegorical approach: by attempting to universalize the quest for peace and fulfillment, by ringing in Muses and ancient philosophers and gabby Stage Managers, by making the planets speak and the dead rise, by stripping away the usually gross, realistic stage decor, he hoped to isolate those fragments of human experience that normally elude us. And he succeeded—by accomplishing what he claimed people were unable to do: to arrest and to preserve those fleeting, fragmentary, imperfectly perceived moments of life.

Our Town, for instance, was a particularly brazen achievement, especially when we consider that he chose to devour an entire town—its history, geography, and politics—and then to engage the entire race of man—from Genesis to the world wars—to give Everyman an even wider berth. From such vast canvases he could select, like a pilot circling at five thousand feet, the high points, the chief landmarks that identify the most salient compulsions and failures that are most common among men.

By abolishing scenery, props, and even plot, and preserving only the most rudimentary acknowledgment of time and space, he plunges us—abruptly—into Grovers Corners, that American idyll, that homely, serene, enduring home town that we feel we all deserve. Nobody rapes or murders in Grovers Corners; there are no bank scandals, no greed, no infidelity; no one is agonizing over his loss of personal identity or the moral devastation that is charring the landscape. A dull town. But wait: exciting things are happening; not earthshaking, merely *important*. People are being born, they are living together, they are falling in love, they are dying. And most important of all: they are *missing most of it*. They have occasional glimpses, to be sure. Dr. Gibbs remarks how he thought he'd run out of things to say to his wife, but hasn't. Young Rebecca innocently reflects on some cosmic geography, tracing, by stages, the ladder that ascends from her bedroom window clear up to God; Emily and George repeat the immutable cycle of life by falling in love; a boy delivers newspapers, blithely unaware that he will die in the war; and Emily, who dies too soon, begs to return so that she might share with the living the secret she now knows about life: that we pay a terrible penalty for mortality, that life moves at such a tragic velocity we are virtually powerless to stop it long enough to discover its aroma and feeling.

Our Town is not a play; it is a series of lyric impressions that try to weave a melancholy tune. And despite what the innumerable high school productions have done to the reputation of the play, despite the injuries inflicted on it by adolescent performers and myopic critics (who themselves are perfect examples of the imperfect perception

Wilder is discussing), the play is a triumphant amalgam of both the expressionist and allegorical traditions as well as a testament to the essential nobility and profundity of simple human experience.

True, Wilder hangs on hard to a middle-class ethic that does, indeed, resist change. But I don't really mind that at all. In a period of drift that taxes our emotional patience and cerebral fortitude, it's most reassuring to rediscover Grovers Corners and to come in safe—if only briefly—from the storm.

Wilder is equally successful with *Skin of Our Teeth*. The play is one of the more strikingly original dramatic compositions in the modern American catalog, largely because of the incredible allegory he is trying to construct: man's eternal struggle for existence. The message gets murky at times because of the thick appliqué of self-conscious devices that fill us with puzzlement and wonder.

For example, a news broadcast, accompanied by lantern slides, immediately sets the cosmic tone of the play.

> Freeport, Long Island. The sun rose this morning at 6:32 A.M. This gratifying event was first reported by Mrs. Dorothy Stetson of Freeport, Long Island, who promptly telephoned the Mayor. The Society for Affirming the End of the World at once went into a special session and postponed the arrival of that Event for twenty-four hours.
>
> New York City. The X Theatre. During the daily cleaning of this theatre a number of lost objects were collected. . . . Among those objects found today was a wedding ring, inscribed: To Eva from Adam, Genesis II:18. The ring will be restored to the owner or owners, if their credentials are satisfactory.
>
> Excelsior, New Jersey. The home of Mr. George Antrobus, the inventor of the wheel. . . . This is his

home, a commodious seven-room house, conveniently situated near a public school, a Methodist church, and a firehouse; it is right handy to the A. and P. Mr. Antrobus himself. He comes of very old stock and has made his way up from next to nothing. It is reported that he was once a gardener, but left that situation under circumstances that have been variously reported.

It's hard to miss the point. The mixture of biblical beginnings with suburban comforts and imminent global destruction with tidy domestic securities creates the kind of suspended animation and universal breadth that Wilder requires to launch a tale of the cyclic fall and rise of mankind.

Once the tone is set, it's relatively easy to demolish one traditional stage convention after another. The Antrobus family maid, Lily Sabina—who derives her name from Lillith, Adam's first wife in rabbinical literature, and from the Sabine women—freely addresses the audience, sharing their confusion and dismay over such a heady dramatic theme:

> I hate this play and every word in it. As for me, I don't understand a single word of it, anyway—all about the troubles the human race has gone through, there's a subject for you. . . . Oh—why can't we have plays like we used to have—Peg O' My Heart, and Smilin' Through, and The Bat, good entertainment with a message you can take home with you?

Clearly, Wilder is anticipating the reaction to his novel experiment and offered Lily's remarks as both gentle mockery of an audience's limitations and a whimsical admission of the outrageous stunts he is trying to pull off.

In quick succession, a mammoth and a dinosaur creep

in, refugees from the Ice Age, to warm themselves by the Antrobus fire. Compositions of stage figures are called for that reproduce, according to a stage direction, a "tableau by Raphael." Judge Moses strolls in (wearing a skullcap) as does Homer (as a blind beggar with a guitar) and we are treated to recitations in Hebrew and Greek. The three Muses appear: Miss E. (for Erato, lyric and love poetry), Miss M. (Melpomone, for tragedy) and Miss T. (Thalia, for comic or pastoral poetry). And by the end of Act I, while Gladys is praying to God to avert disaster, Sabina asks the audience for help: "Will you please start handing up your chairs? We'll need everything for the fire. Save the human race.—Ushers, will you pass the chairs up here? Thank you." From the back of the auditorium comes the sound of chairs being ripped from their moorings, and ushers begin hurrying down the aisles to hand them over to Sabina.

These Olsen and Johnson techniques puzzled many critics and offended others. We can certainly understand why. Not because the theme or techniques were irrelevant. Indeed, world events in 1942, when the play opened, raised questions of man's survival and the chaos men were about to plunge into that made Wilder's treatment seem very relevant indeed. Rather, critics were maddened largely because they had never seen such brazen theatricality that so precariously bordered on being facetious. A few of the more cynical critics even attacked Wilder for the naïve righteousness of his vision; that is, that man *deserves* another chance. What I think really troubled the skeptics, however, was Wilder's bravura handling, and crystallizing, of both the expressionist and allegorical traditions. He had found the means—albeit they were both sophisticated (in theme) and childlike (in devices) that welded the traditions together in a way that had never been seen before. Wilder was insisting that natural and man-made devastation (the expressionist mode) in no way contradicts, and will certainly in no way thwart, man's efforts to continue his perilous search for survival (the allegorical mode). To prove this thesis, he was obliged to invoke vivid symbols and to hurl them at the audience at a velocity it could scarcely accommodate, as a means of creating the sense of the panorama of existence.

It was Brooks Atkinson who most accurately assessed the real merit and achievement of the play:

> The breezy form gives the impression that mankind carries forward its ancient and honorable traditions unconsciously in the midst of squalor, vulgarity and muddle—never aware of its spiritual valor. In this way, the slapstick provides form and perspective. [The play] has intellectual stature. It is an expression of faith by a man of knowledge and principle.

That's the key: an "expression of faith." And those who fail to find it have allowed their membership as optimists to lapse and are just guilty enough of imperfect awareness to miss seeing the forest for the trees.

For Tennessee Williams it was considerably harder to give voice to such an expression of faith because, for him, even the skin on our teeth had been scraped away, and "our town" was the interior jungle of the soul. Although more attuned to failure than to triumph, more content with traditional playwrighting methods than with conscious experiment, more concerned with the private poetry of pain than with cosmic disorders, Williams is as totally committed to the expressionism-allegory tradition as is Wilder. Which is by way of saying that he employs highly selective symbols of human distress to trace the pilgrimage of the errant soul.

A number of labels have been pinned on Williams, all of them noteworthy for their ambiguity. He's been called a "poetic realist," a "sensual realist," "the poet of the damned," and a "moral symbolist." As with any tags, they make the product look tempting without necessarily defining its value. And there is substantial value to Williams that the labels only hint at; for despite such sensational morsels as rape, homosexuality, cannibalism, adultery, and castration, there is at the heart of all his plays the outcry of the deeply wounded moralist, a terror-stricken lament for what seems to be society's conspiracy to erase human innocence. Recall Nonno's poem in *Night of the Iguana:*

> *O Courage, could you not as well*
> *Select a second place to dwell,*
> *Not only in that golden tree,*
> *But in the frightened heart of me?*

Williams has been in the business of playwrighting long enough, and has proved himself consistent enough in the development of certain themes so that we might very properly take his vision of the world quite seriously. It's an unhappy vision, one that reflects the infinite distortions and inversions of human values that tend to stifle most of the old platitudes about love, loyalty, personal freedom, and sexual liberation. Such a vision has developed in Williams a special compassion for "the people who are not meant to win," the lost people—as the *Time* critic put it—"the odd, the strange, the difficult people—fragile spirits, who lack talons for the jungle." As a consequence they are *incomplete* people who are compelled to thrash about in bizarre ways as a means of seeking escape from the tentative and inconclusive nature of their lives; rather like the hysterical scream when you're lost in a dark cave. One of Williams' recent biographers (Benjamin Nelson) suggests rightly that we may not agree with this total loss of wholeness in the universe, that we may even reject it. "What we cannot do," Nelson observes, "is to deny it."

Mr. Williams has had to live with a double dilemma.

On the one hand, the puritan instinct in conflict with human corruption; on the other, a fragmented and chaotic universe in conflict with the intuition and skill of an orderly dramatist. Williams not only has found the means to reconcile the moral and aesthetic division in both his art and life, but has been able to convert the psychic tensions these divisions produce into a source of uncommonly high dramatic energy. As a result Williams is, without doubt, the most gifted theatre writer in this country. We can agree, without reservation, with Brooks Atkinson's estimate:

> By the incantation of words, which combine lyricism and naturalism, he creates images of life that actors can express with great force on the stage. He has the elusive rhythms of the theatre in his blood. Whether his images are attractive or odious, they cannot be denied, because Mr. Williams creates them vividly. Writing from the inside out, like Chekhov, he can make something tangible out of moods and dreams.

It is his first dilemma—the sensualist in combat with the puritan—that provokes the most interest. In the true spirit of the allegorist, Williams forces his characters to travel over an eerie landscape, a moral obstacle course full of the spiritual traps and fleshly aberrations that reveal the profound divisions in human nature. When sifted out, virtually all his plays—from *The Glass Menagerie* to *The Milk Train Doesn't Stop Here Anymore* to the recent bill of Off-Broadway one-actors—the most elemental conflicts emerge: the primitive struggle between God and the Devil, between love and death, between light and dark, between innocence and corruption, and between illusion and reality. Here it is again: the ambivalence, the compulsion to voyage coupled with the longing to be home, the romantic dream of a lost paradise, a nirvana of rest, that promises the kind of total fulfillment, total engagement with the full range of sensual experiences that life promises but never seems to deliver.

These deep divisions—familiar enough to all of us—and the desire to close the gap between them, made D. H. Lawrence a magnetic force for Williams. From Lawrence, he drew support for what he believed to be one of the serious consequences of the gap: the starkly lonely condition of man. As late as 1955, he wrote:

> It is a lonely idea, a lonely condition, so terrifying to think of that we usually don't. And so we talk to each other, write and wire each other, call each other short and long distance across land and sea, clasp hands with each other at meetings and at parting, fight each other and even destroy each other. As a character in a play once said, "We're all of us sentenced to solitary confinement inside our skins." Personal lyricism is the outcry of prisoner to prisoner from the cell in solitary where he is confined for the duration of his life.

This ambivalence, then, is a source of loneliness. That's expected. What's worse is that it's a form of punishment, a kind of terrible penalty for being part of a vindictive society that makes a man a conspirator whether he likes it or not.

Being lonely—and thus incapacitated—reinforced another of Williams' notions that was also derived from Lawrence: the idea of the writer forcibly altering society, making it mend its way, as a means of finding release from a stifling prudery. In *I Rise in Flames, Cried the Phoenix*, the character representing D. H. Lawrence says:

> Why do I want to write? Because I'm an artist . . . What is an artist? A man who loves life too intensely, a man who loves life till he hates her and has to strike

out with his fist. . . . I want to stretch out the long
sweet arms of my art and embrace the whole world!
But it isn't enough to go out to the world with love.
And so I doubled my fist and I struck and I struck.
Words weren't enough. . . . I had to have color, too.
I took to paint and I painted the way that I wrote!
Fiercely, without any shame! *This* is life, I told them,
life is like *this!* Wonderful! Dark! Terrific!

The speech is full of the Williams code: the intensely
romanticized view of life; the selfless giving of one's mind
and body; the sense of outrage over the world's indifference
and rigidity; the final recourse to violence. And if we treat
the last three words literally rather than figuratively, we
have even a closer translation of the code: "wonderful"—
full of awe and astonishment; "dark"—full of unforeseen
threats that challenge the spirit and energy of the artist;
"terrific"—full of terror. In other words, Williams is seeing
life *itself,* in its natural course of events, as a necessarily
ambivalent experience; and that to live it fully, we must
be prepared to accept both terror and wonder, decadence
and purity, love (as intense human contact) and death (as
lack of this contact). Not since O'Neill—about the only
other American playwright with whom any comparisons
can be made—has a playwright more boldly declared the
essentially primeval climate in which man pretends he does
not live.

In the actual practice of translating vision into action
on the stage, Williams has had no choice but to turn to
poetic instruments. The wickedness of the world cannot be
merely described, it has to be illustrated. And to compress
so much evil into two hours of playing time, it's necessary
to transform the assorted evils into walking metaphors,
surround them with provocative and tenacious symbols,
and then let them speak in the emotionally charged ca-

dences humans invariably speak in when gripped by fear or despair.

As metaphors, the characters operate brilliantly. To underscore the plight of the people "who cannot win," Williams shows them in desperate flight. The metaphor is escape; or where escape is impossible—as it usually is—then concealment will do, repression will do, anesthesia (in the form of drugs or alcohol) will do. (That last outpost for human gargoyles that serves as the setting for *Night of the Iguana* is the epitome of this.) What precipitates flight is, of course, reality; or more precisely—and more frustratingly—a reality that has lost its credibility. Reality jars these characters; it hurts them; it magnifies the gap, the psychic division in their souls that is already calamitous enough. Alma, in *Summer and Smoke,* devours sleeping pills to avoid dealing with her own sexual repressions; Brick, in *Cat on a Hot Tin Roof,* retreats in alcohol to overcome a homosexual episode earlier in his life; Laura invests herself in a fragile world of glass as protection against the permanent disenchantments of the real world; and Blanche, the thin, neurasthenic, romancing, pathetic spinster, surrounds herself with pink lampshades, cheap finery, and hallucinations of a social grandeur that never existed.

Even if the act of flight deepens self-betrayal, it must be done. To have no role to play, no mask to hold up to deaden the shock of the real world and its harsh inquisitiveness, is to surrender the remaining particles of human identity. This is a crucial aspect of Williams' moral philosophy. Although his characters are in retreat, in active flight from untenable truths about themselves, they are hanging on to life as hard as they are running. Not the kind of life we'd wish for ourselves or our children, to be sure; but where there's life, there's hope. Maybe not in Blanche, Alma, or the ex-Reverend Shannon, but in Williams.

To support these metaphors of flight, Williams invokes the most bald and abundant lexicon of symbols since O'Neill: hobbyhorses and crutches, goats and snakeskin jackets, iguanas (who chew their own tails off to escape) and carnivorous birds, funeral limousines and Adonis-like Christ-figures—all of them transfiguring the underlying ambivalence of good and evil into poetic realities on the stage.

In *Camino Real,* his symbol-making takes on massive proportions. The hero is named Kilroy, an American wanderer; prominent in the stage setting is a phoenix painted on silk; on one side of the mythical city square is the Sieta Mares Hotel, on the other, Skid Row. Between them a great flight of stairs mounts the ancient wall to a sort of archway that leads away to "Terra Incognita," "a wasteland between the walled town and the distant perimeter of snow-topped mountains," as the stage directions read.

Having set the symbolic-allegorical tone so solidly, it's no surprise to see other fictional and legendary figures parade through. Here is Don Quixote still declaring for Truth, Valor, and Duty and not finding them; here is an abstract figure called merely the Survivor, who stumbles into the square, tries to find drinking water, and is shot by the guards; here is the Dreamer, also dragged away; here is Kilroy himself, in dungarees and a prizefighter's belt bearing the word "Champ." Having been robbed, he can't get into the hotel either, and is informed that the only way out is to climb the stairs, a notoriously fearful journey. Faltering and afraid, Kilroy is bolstered by no other than Lord Byron who proclaims:

> There is a time for departure even when there's no place to go! I'm going to look for one now. I'm sailing to Athens. The old pure music will come to me again. Of course on the other hand I may hear only

the little noises of insects in the grass. . . . But I am sailing to Athens! *Make voyages! Attempt them!* —there's nothing else.

Kilroy makes the attempt, but fails—twice. Lacking courage, and susceptible to sensual pleasures, his escape is never consummated. He does, however, get to enjoy a symbolic resurrection, only to capitulate to the same sins again. But Williams has not quite registered his message yet. When, at the end of the play, Don Quixote returns and asks Kilroy if he has any plans, the reply is that he is "thinking of—going *on* from—*here!*" Having suffered from the human vanities of lust and material gain, he can now —maybe—mount the stairway.

What occurs in the final moments of the action occurs in no other Williams play. As Broussard puts it:

> Examined comparatively, *Camino Real* becomes the playwright's prescription for the character failures presented in his other plays. This decade's most prolific playwright . . . since O'Neill may yet come to write of resurrections.

He did, indeed, try again. The character of Chris (add the "t") in *Milk Train* is called upon to dispense physical and spiritual regeneration. But the allegory is so muddled that Christ seems to turn into Apollo, and we're not quite sure where we are.

But in *Camino Real,* he rolls into one bundle the metaphoric and symbolic images of physical need and spiritual despair that have become the currency of poetic naturalism; he laces together the expressionist-allegoric traditions to enjoy the free technique of the former, and the search syndrome of the latter.

To Thornton Wilder, man is drawn upward in his search. To Tennessee Williams, man is drawn downward. As a pair, they serve the theatre as mapmakers of the principal roadways of ancient and modern man: the ascent to heaven, the descent into hell.

To Arthur Miller, however, man is split down the middle and drawn in two lateral directions at once, leaving a terrible void where his innocence, moral judgment, and social responsibility used to be.

Imbedded deeply and firmly in all the works of Miller is the singular theme: one man is—indeed, *must be*—the bondsman for all men. There is neither theology nor demonology in this theme; the upper or nether regions have little claim on or are of much interest to the figures who populate Miller's plays or the ideas that occupy Miller's thought. His landscape is the real world, a world in which man is a social creature, obsessed by the fact that there is a double mortgage on him: the debt he owes to himself, and the one he owes to the greater world of men around him. The Miller hero has in other words, both an objective and subjective existence; both existences make fierce demands on him which he often cannot meet. To complicate matters, the hero may lack a clear understanding of his identity and function as an insular unit (either as one man or as "family") while, at the same time, failing to fully accept or completely reject the image of himself that is a product of his society's values and prejudices. Torn between what he wants as a man and what is expected of him as a social integer, he fails to find comfort in either role, and is transformed into Everyman, wandering through a no-man's-land of incoherent desires and obscure objectives. The magnitude of this no-man's-land may change from play to play (Joe Keller's back yard, Eddie Carbon's waterfront neighborhood, John Proctor's hostile village, Willy Loman's "Territory," or Quentin's tortured soul) but its threatening atmosphere remains the same.

The schizoid nature of human existence was embodied

with great clarity in Miller's first successful play, *All My Sons* (1947). It's a well-known work by now, thoroughly squeezed of all its meaning. The title itself expresses the central theme: Joe Keller's responsibility is to a world larger than the comfortable bourgeois isolation and ethic of his private life. The creaky, melodramatic plot (war profiteering, cracked engine blocks, the suicide of the son and the father) tends to conceal the real war going on in American society; the battle between the memory of an old morality and "practicality." "Sure, be honest," says Joe, "but a man's got to make a buck."

What gives the play stature, Harold Clurman suggests, is Miller's reluctance to place the blame for men like Joe on "the system"; on a ruthless, impersonal disfiguring corruption of ideals known as "getting along with the world." There can be no shifting of guilt, no evasion of the burden of individual responsibility. In fact, the man who blames all his woes on society is both a weakling and a coward and deserves whatever punishment he gets.

So it's not society he blames—which is, after all, a composite of the tacit and formal understandings among men —but rather the well-meaning, kindly, loving, overprotective, safe status quo; the deadly middle-class ethic that unconsciously distorts a man's values so that he can keep the ethic as safe, loving, and kindly as a sanctuary. Clurman argues, in fact, that the real villain of the piece is Joe Keller's wife, the "little woman," the innocent keeper of the snakepit. "I'm like everybody else now," the son says bitterly to the mother, "I'm practical now. You made me practical." And she answers: "But you have to be." An empty piece of wisdom, and one calculated to reinforce the primacy of the family as the final excuse for any public action.

In *Death of a Salesman,* Miller plunges directly into one of the more corrupting of the American Dreams. Having dealt with one kind of perverse security—the family influence—he is now ready for a larger kind—the myth of success through selling not a product, but a soul.

The death of Willy comes about—not because of a venal, capitalistic society (Miller is sticking to his guns; society is not the culprit), not because of Miller's presumed leftist leanings, but because of the total, ultimate, and inevitable breakdown of the whole concept of salesmanship (selling things, selling ideas, selling self) in our society.

Death of a Salesman quite properly falls into the moral-allegorical tradition, freely using expressionistic technique to highlight the pivotal crises in a man's life. It's truly a morality play, in the most medieval sense of the term: the reworking of a universal challenge to man's identity and souls, set in abstract terms yet premised on tangible realities; the Deadly Sins have been replaced by the Deadly Values that entrap and betray the hero.

In the last analysis, however, it's not the breakdown of the selling concept, not the self-indulgent moralizing, not the political or ideological overtones that move us. It is the pathos of Willy and his patent medicine prescriptions for life, his cliché-images of happiness and success, his futile acts to find a soil to flourish in, his inflated—but entirely understandable—paternalism, his utter bewilderment as his dreams, his children, his faulty car, his whipped cheese, and his hopeless garden all coil about him, like a noxious gas, and finally smother him. We are moved and stunned by Willy because we are kin to Willy and products of the same tyrannical myths, the same fatuous, tempting ideologies that pulled him under. And we mourn Willy mostly because we are powerless to help him.

Willy never learns, he never knew what hit him. But then, neither do we—as a frail, mortal race—ever learn either.

If poetry is, in essence, the magnification and distillation of human experience, then *Death of a Salesman* is one of the great poetic plays of the 20th century.

With *The Crucible* (1953), the story of a man's will to

bear his private guilt privately, Miller places himself in a precarious position. The artist in him seems to be at odds with the militant protester. Having announced in a 1954 essay that America was going through a kind of group therapy that demanded the declaration of each man's *mea culpa, The Crucible* surely seems brewed out of the same conviction. And to a large extent it was: *The Crucible's* portrait of Salem's mass hysteria in which the proclamation of personal guilt becomes a public virtue is surely analogous to the McCarthy-type witch-hunts. Certainly characters such as the villainous Danforth, the ambitious Parris, the greedy Putnam, the envious Abigail indicate Miller's sense of wrath against those who use the crying-out technique, who destroy others to serve their own interests.

But in the character of John Proctor, and in Miller's reluctance to reduce character to a mere social specimen, we sense that the artist is winning out over the protestor. Miller deliberately creates a romantic hero, a sentient being, who can—unlike Joe and Willy—accurately perceive what's going on around him, weigh correctly the stakes that are involved, and struggle to retain the marks of private guilt as a personal problem, one that gives him identity and character.

Perhaps Proctor came off better than Miller intended, for we find ourselves caring for him as a man rather than as a symbol. Remember, it is the resolution of a moral crisis (the charge of adultery), not a political or ideological one, that clears the air for him, freeing him to reject the false confession of consorting with witches and then use— or surrender—his life as he sees fit. It's a kind of freedom that transcends, finally, the inferior and temporal calamities of localized witch-hunting and public panic; it's a freedom that asserts that the dignity (i.e., identity) of a man is his primary reason for life. John Proctor *could* have signed that paper and submitted to the final, downward humiliation, to the anti-heroic, existential, absurdist deflation. It might have scored some good points for our side, showing an ultimate consequence or two of the destructive power of self-appointed judges. But Proctor does *not* sign; and this act becomes humanitarian rather than existential. And if it is an abstract affirmation of individual human privilege, then the evil that precipitates this act is similarly abstract; i.e., *any* shackling of the human spirit. The allegorist remains stronger in Miller than the agitator.

In *After the Fall,* Miller tries to materialize a search allegory out of insubstantial materials: the memories and anxieties of a man who fears he has strayed too far from Eden. In his foreword to the work, Miller makes clear where he stands vis-à-vis the world around him. His view, he writes, "does not look toward social or political ideas as the creators of violence, but into the nature of the human being himself," and that to become "himself" is an act of becoming aware of his sinfulness. Throughout the millennia, argues Miller, the human being has struggled to pacify his own destructive impulses—his peculiar form of sin— and to find instead "a clear view of his own responsibility for his life." Such a view cannot be obtained until a man puts himself on trial and stands accused by his own conscience, his own values, and his own acquiescence to those violent impulses.

That's what Miller says *After the Fall* is, a trial; and the hero will stand either guilty or innocent of joining with the biblical Cain in deflowering the Garden of Eden.

The "business of the day," Miller concludes in the manner of the avowed allegorist, is the "mindless flight from our own actual experience, a flight which empties out the soul."

There's something vaguely beatific and unctuous in these pronouncements. That's all right; what's not all right is that the Olympian and Solomon-like tone permeates the whole play and is more often used to disguise the sweeping up of some leftover rubble in Mr. Miller's heart than to articulate any fresh or objective theme.

A note of real disappointment may be detected here. The play, finally, is about as exciting as an old man taking out his teeth at night. In fairness to Miller, we are promised a startling dissection of a man's soul, but we receive, as one critic put it, "a documentary of one man's life with the man himself addressing the audience in a blurred rhetoric whose dominant note sounded like self-apology. . . . One squirmed for the playwright who was throwing away his human rights of privacy."

Miller, of course, protested that Quentin was not Arthur; that Maggie was not Marilyn; that a cold first wife was not Arthur's cold first wife; that the foreign girl Holga was not really the foreign photographer, Inge, who moved into Miller's life in Connecticut and later married him; that Quentin's appearance before an Un-American Committee was not Arthur's, that Quentin's foreign-born father who lost a sizable business in the Depression wasn't Arthur's foreign-born father who lost a sizable business in the Depression; that Quentin's brother (Dan) wasn't Arthur's own brother who also stayed home to help the father reestablish the business; and so on. So many important factual parallels are undeniable, Leonard Moss points out in a fascinating study of the biographical and literary allusion in the play, that any protest on Miller's part is gratuitous. But under the aura of the mighty Miller name, of a theatre especially constructed and designed for him, of a high-tension cast of actors, of a distinguished director, and of the whole thrill of a new concept of American repertory theatre coming into existence, it was hoped that the blatant analogies could be forgiven.

And they almost could be. There's nothing fundamentally awry with the theme: a man's fall from innocence, and his continuing search for a rationale he can live by. Nor is there anything fundamentally wrong with autobiography. All playwrights are, at their core, biographers of their own experiences. But what transforms a work from an overheated *report* to a coherently dramatic *reflection* is a kind of experiential osmosis. The actual happenings in the life of a writer aren't ever as important as how those happenings modify his views of life around him. To wince and yelp with pain will help soften the agony of one man; but to suffer pain, recover from it, and then *use* what you have learned in order to understand *all* men is the function of the artist. It is known as artistic selection and decorum.

Mr. Miller is guilty of abusing his artistic prerogatives and of exploiting his own preeminence as an established writer to use the stage as a private megaphone. And I intend not the slightest air of patronage when I say: It's too bad, but it's nice he got it out of his system.

Well, so much for an incomplete account of the three major allegorists of the 20th century. All three, as we've seen, are marked by powerful visions of the world, and strong biases toward it. All three have, at least *once* in their careers, found the key to that mysterious amalgam of form and idea that makes for memorable theatre. All three have contributed character images to the American folk experience that will serve, whether we like it or not, as touchstones for future historians. And all three are, despite their dramatizations of the overly naïve or overly disfigured propensities of man, believers in the ultimate justification of man as a rational creature. And all three have had the courage to illustrate what hell we might have to go through to reach that rational state.

They are in search of Tinker Bell.

vi

The Birth of Tinker Bell

I wish the plot were more tidy. I wish, in this final chapter, I could describe how Tinker Bell would be invited back to the bosom of the American theatre. Being of a charitable and loving disposition, she would return, gracefully accepting apologies from the paranoid practitioners of the commercial theatre, from the erstwhile tragedians and the armchair psychiatrists, from the dramaturgically lame poets, and from the self-annointed moralists who swept her aside in order to ruminate undisturbed over fractured human ethics. It would be good to have Tinker Bell return, forgive everyone, and embrace the American theatre at the final fade.

Such an ending, however, would be not only unrealistic but also impossible. The plain truth seems to be that the Tinker Bell we have been so lovingly pursuing and so vigorously mourning probably never existed. As a symbol of sustained dramatic vision, viable imagination, and national character, Tinker Bell has been hardly more than a paradigm, a piece of nostalgic speculation, a lovely dream of a theatrical (and cultural) grandeur; in short, an abortive myth that, like so much of the aesthetic criteria of the American theatre, is a vague amalgam of imported theory and racial memory.

An even plainer truth is that the American theatre itself does not exist. There is theatre in America, to be sure; but it is not an American Theatre. If anything, it is a variegated, and heterogeneous cluster of artistic monopolies and vested interests that operate under different labels: professional, amateur, educational, and community. There is, we are told, the kind of strength and excitement in this artistic diversity that is similar to the "melting pot" image of early 20th-century America: the robust strains of a dozen national traditions fusing together into a distinctive cultural force. At this point similarity ends abruptly. Despite the compulsive lip service given to matters of a unified view of the nature of theatre art, to the questing after uniform standards of teaching, writing, and performance, and to the essential connection between American theatre and American life, the various monopolies and interests remain largely insular if not, indeed, hostile toward one another. The crusty professional retains his skepticism toward the Ivory Tower; the professor is horrified at the creative waste and despair of the commercial stage; the community theatre buff, unsupported by university subsidies, paralyzed by the indifferent support of the general citizenry, and awed by the hit-or-miss syndrome of the legitimate theatre, is set adrift to fume at all parties and to struggle to achieve respectability as a social agency and glamor as a producer of hit—if slightly warmed over—plays.

There is nothing new about the insular and divisive nature of the theatre in America, about its determination to remain a cellular rather than organic cultural force. Sporadic efforts during the early 20th century to find a theme or metaphor that would serve to crystallize the disparate movements within the theatre were generally unsuccessful. The intensive Agit-Prop (Agitation-Propaganda) activity of Labor Front movements in the 1920's developed a heady proposal: to bind the nation into a network of militant theatre groups whose singular theme would be the restoration of dignity and power to the Worker. The network never fully developed because the social reforms of New Deal legislation, the threat of impending prosperity as war clouds materialized, and the Stalin-Hitler pact (which erased much of the Communist stamp from the Labor Theatre) made Agit-Prop seem utterly gratuitous.

The Federal Theatre Project, a major program of the Works Progress Administration, tried for four years (1935 to 1939) to prove that a great national wealth—the artist of the theatre—was being dissipated. Through elaborately organized regional "Units" the Federal Theatre not only put actors, writers, directors, singers, dancers, and musicians back on a payroll, but also sought to cultivate regional identity by developing—in musico-dramatic forms —traits and attitudes that were most characteristic of a given geographic area. The sorry fate of the Federal Theatre has already been described.

As late as the 1940's, the search for an idea that would help to polarize the nation's disparate cultural energies took the form of the American Repertory Theatre, undertaken by two visionary ladies, Eva Le Gallienne and Cheryl Crawford. Their premise was simple: high quality classical plays at low box-office prices for the entire country. The country liked the premise, but it quickly became apparent that enthusiastic support was not enough to defray high production and traveling costs or to inject a theatrical virility into the academic acting style of Miss Le Gallienne's actors. The American Repertory Theatre collapsed after barely two years of operation.

By the time ANTA (American National Theatre and Academy) introduced its "Theatre 40" plan in the 1950's —a plan to establish forty regional centers for professional theatre around the country—an entrenched skepticism prevailed, and the plan never left the ground.

Labor, Federal, Repertory, and Regional concepts of organization and production could not reprieve a theatre that, for 240 years, had been condemned to a commercial, derivative, and transitory existence. The plaintive early 19th-century pleas for a free, flourishing, intrinsically American theatre voiced by the playwright-historian William Dunlap, and reechoed periodically ever since, were drowned out by the clamorous support Americans gave to English, French, and German playwrights, by the prolonged ovations accorded foreign stars, acting companies, and producers, and by the shuffling sound of American playwrights' feet on wooden gangplanks as the writers headed abroad.

The few efforts to celebrate native resources resulted in trivia: garish melodramas of frontier life, of plantation life, of big city life, of "high life" in voguish circles, and of life in the Secret Service of Civil War days. In sum, native resources degenerated into the *Margaret Fleming* syndrome that infected Eugene O'Neill and insinuated itself into the dramatic styles of virtually every major playwright of the 20th century. Like a stifling shroud, the "American tradition" of dramatic composition—this ubiquitous sludge of melodramatic half-truths and baldly inflated passions—had one obvious effect: it preserved the notion of an inferior theatre in America.

To forestall any misunderstanding, I should point out that I am not defiling melodrama as such. It is an honorable dramatic method, a potent means of swiftly capitalizing dramatic crises and human confrontations; it escalates ideas, by techniques of suspense, surprise, and sudden reversals, transforming abstractions into sentient and vivid episodes. Only when melodrama is undisciplined in its application or when the purely sensational aspects of human dilemmas are presented does melodrama begin to debase and obscure the dramatic vision it is trying to develop.

In view of the inherited traditions of a hand-me-down, redundant, and melodramatic theatre, of the failure to believe in and to promote native resources, and of the inevitable growth of artistic enclaves as pocket protectorates of special interests, the notion of an American Theatre seems utterly untenable.

Perhaps it is time for a new and very strict accounting of the American theatre. Perhaps it would be more profitable to abandon the notion of theatre as a metaphor of a singular national experience, and to think of the theatre in America as we think of American society itself, as a pluralistic phenomenon—i.e., think of it as *many* theatres. Perhaps, if our accounting is scrupulously accurate, we'll discover that our national theatre isn't the theatre at all, but the motion picture. With the technology, financial resources, means of distribution, and performing centers that the film industry enjoys, it long ago surpassed the legitimate stage as a maker and preserver of popular myths. Perhaps our national theatre is, or will shortly become, television. It's hardly inconceivable that this might occur in view of the programing resources of the major educational television networks.

That television and the film happily forego offering the living presence of the actor may be, after all, inconsequential. Who says that a theatrical experience *requires* in-the-flesh actors? Can this requirement be proved? Haven't distinguished theoreticians, most notably Edward Gordon Craing, proposed that the live actor be replaced by puppets, reminding us that a number of great foreign cultures (especially Oriental and African) have embodied their most profound racial experiences in puppets and marionettes? The devoted and sophisticated playgoers might argue in favor of the live actor, but this suggests support for the argument by an elite group, only *one* kind of audience. Couldn't the motion picture and television deliver quality drama—if they were so disposed—to a phenomenally large audience on a maximally efficient, economically sound basis?

If the theatre in America lacks the economic sagacity, the aesthetic insight, and the sustained social vision to make it a unified and prophetic force in the lives of the American public, then let it go. It has been noticeably lacking in these three traits for nearly three centuries.

If the theatre in America has been unable to resolve its philosophical responsibilities, its poetic responsibilities, and its moral responsibilities without retreating, like a college sophomore with a term paper, into facile, ready-made, and derivative solutions, then let it go. There are well-established agencies that have been dealing successfully with philosophic, poetic, and moral issues for years.

If those who are its principal apologists, critics, and performers cannot foreswear their professional myopia long enough to unite in an exploration of the matrix of the American national character, and to rediscover the primal humane and social fibers of that matrix as a preliminary step toward revitalizing the fundamental myths and rituals that are most consonant with American life, then let the theatre go. Let it become, honestly and openly, the Pleasure Pit for voyeurism, emotional ennui, and intellectual complacence. Who needs it? Who needs the overpriced tickets, the naïve aesthetic posturing, the voguish imitations of hit plays or hit theories, and the numbing mixture of cynicism and amateurism that seems to characterize *all* the manifestations of the American theatre?

Indeed, let it go and then begin to take hope in the fact that the American theatre really hasn't died at all; it simply hasn't been born yet. Death assumes some form of life—independent, self-contained, and purposeful life. For nearly three centuries the American theatre has lived by transfusions of foreign dramatic idioms and styles, fed intravenously on nourishment administered by an Adolphe Appia, a Sigmund Freud, a Friedrich Nietzsche, a Max Reinhardt, a Luigi Pirandello, a Bertolt Brecht, and a Peter Weiss. Such transfusions and nourishment have been most beneficial, supplying the American legitimate and educational stages with artistic concepts, concrete models of theatrical forms, and fresh critical dogma. Supported by extra-territorial influences, the American theatre has not been dead; it simply has not yet found a life of its own.

Only now, a little past the midpoint of the 20th century, are indications beginning to appear that suggest that the theatre in America might become an American Theatre. After three centuries of playing with the neighbor's toys, of eagerly accepting a spoonfeeding of forms and ideas, of learning to walk and talk by direct imitation, and of trying everyone's patience, theatre may be through its prepuberty period and its healthy adolescence starting.

There are numerous signs of this development. As one might expect, some are stronger and clearer than others; indeed, they seem to fall into three categories: firm signs, weak signs, and *anti* signs. All merit brief examination here because they represent—at the very least—token gestures of a maturing attitude toward theatre art and—at the very most—the beginnings of a significant reawakening of a nation's cultural conscience. None of the signs make absolute promises about anything, but by their volume and scope there is reason to believe that there has occurred in the 20th-century American theatre a vital and widespread zeal to reexamine the fundamental tenets and objectives of the theatre and to establish those programs that will most dramatically reconnect the potential of theatre art and the promise of American life. Indeed, this new zeal has something of the aspect of the rush for land precipitated by the Homestead Act; but in the theatre, the rush is for carving out great quadrants of culture in the fields of professional, community, and university drama.

Of the various firm signs, perhaps the most singular development is the unembarrassed effort to restore a high order of professionalism to the preparation for and the practice of theatre art. There is a disturbing irony in this effort. That an acknowledged profession must behave in a manner that certifies its professionalism suggests the low public and self-esteem in which theatre people have been held. This is neither new nor surprising when we recall that since the days of the ancient Roman theatre, of the 15th-century commedia dell' arte, of the Elizabethan theatre, the actor's lot has been neither happy nor approved, that the aura of vagabond, charlatan, and oddball clings, with unnecessary tenacity, to the performing artist.

Fortunately, the new professionalism that the theatre is pursuing is concerned less with the traditional image of the itinerant player than it is with clarifying the sense of cultural responsibility of the art form itself. By advocating such notions as the need for residential theatre centers spread throughout the country, the need to solicit public and private funds to support the identification and training of new playwrights, and the need to somehow close the rift in American college and universities that has traditionally separated specialized preprofessional training for the stage from the generalist approach of a liberal arts experience, the new professionalism has initiated a series of attacks on the American cultural Establishment as a means of both probing for its weakness and supplying it with vital rationales for its own existence.

A major front of these attacks has been the dozen or more American communities that have witnessed, in the past ten to fifteen years, the establishment and growth of full-time professional theatres: Baltimore (Center Stage),

Seattle (Repertory Theatre), Philadelphia (Theater of the Living Arts), Boston (The Charles Playhouse), San Diego (Actors Quarter Theater), Milwaukee (Fred Miller Theater), Dallas (Theater Center), Houston (Alley Theater), Los Angeles (UCLA Theater Group), Minneapolis (Tyrone Guthrie Theater), Oklahoma City (Mummers), San Francisco (Actor's Workshop), Washington, D.C. (Arena Stage), and Memphis (Front Street Theater). I suspect I have omitted a number of others.

Compared to the provincial theaters of England or the state-supported playhouses on the European Continent or in the Soviet Union, the movement toward a more intense regionalism in the American theatre seems lean indeed. Still, fourteen professional organizations, permanently attached to the landscape of their respective communities, regularly offering classic, modern, and experimental productions performed by well-trained, seasoned personnel, and representing a new (yet very old) source of civic morale, is a decent enough beginning. When regional theatres number in the hundreds, when they begin to establish—as some have already begun—their own studios for the development of actors, writers, and directors, and when they begin to exploit the network of professional theatre centers by exchanging ideas, personnel, and productions (as art museums do with paintings or ETV stations with taped programs), theatre as an inevitable concomitant of American life might seem a reality.

A second attack by the new professionalism has dealt with the most perplexing question of all: how do you encourage, find, and develop new writers for the stage? A number of solutions have been proposed that have tried to bypass the familiar route of submitting untried plays to largely disinterested producers. The solutions range from silly to superior, but lately they have been characterized chiefly by their abundance; never in the history of the American theatre has such a wide-ranging, intensive effort been made to uncover new writing talent or to mold "old" writers (of poetry or prose fiction) into skilled playwrights. Nowhere else on the globe—with the possible exception of the newly independent nations of Africa—are private individuals, established public institutions, or moneyed foundations beating the bushes in the search for fresh writers "with something to say."

To create a hypothetical case: Young Writer X is profoundly incensed by the world's indifference to his four-act verse play that deals with the perils of conformity. Young Writer X has real ability; he can tell a story through a coherently structured plot, the characters are reasonably fresh and dimensional, and the dialogue is generally less purple (allowing for the provocative nature of the subject) than many others might write. Young Writer X knows that a new spirit of professional concern for writers like himself is abroad on the land. What, exactly, can he *do* about it? If it were twenty, or even fifteen years ago, he could spend a profitable evening or two reorganizing his file of rejection notes from Broadway producers—notes which usually arrive, if at all, anywhere from six months to three years after the submitting of the play.

Now, however, in the 1960's, he has other channels open. He may still need to keep his rejection file handy, but he might send his play to any one of the directors of the new regional theatres. These directors might not appreciate a heavy influx of plays about the perils of conformity, but nearly all the regional theatres have announced policies of producing, or at least looking for, new plays. He might, if his play is accepted by one of the regional theatres, apply to a foundation offering "seed money" to help the theatre defray production costs and to provide traveling money so that Young Writer X can visit the theatre to attend rehearsals and help refine his play. He might apply for a

Schubert Foundation Fellowship, a program that would permit him to go back to school for a Master of Arts degree. At least a dozen institutions now have Schubert Fellows in residence. There will be, of course, the necessity to pursue a program of study, but the primary objective of his year(s) in attendance is to write one or more full-length plays. When written, the plays might even be read by someone at the Schubert office in New York City.

He might attempt to enroll with the New Dramatists Committee in New York. The program is informal, but apprentice writers can come together, exchange observations about the hazards of playcrafting, receive instruction from visiting professional writers and stage directors, and possibly even see part or all of his play "tried out" in a nearby auditorium. He might seek membership in the Playwrights Program of the American Educational Theatre Association. If the play is selected by the program, it will be made available for performance by participating universities and colleges around the country. He might, if he has been writing some short plays while waiting for the big one to be accepted, submit his one-act plays to Messrs. Richard Barr, Clinton Wilder, and Edward Albee at Theatre 1966 (the Cherry Lane Theatre, Off-Broadway). This producing triumvirate has become the principal advocates of the short play, although its members seem to have a propensity for plays about beds and Ping-Pong balls. If Young Writer X has a similar propensity for unorthodox dramatic subjects, Theatre 1966 may be a legitimate outlet for him.

Matters are almost as promising for Older Writer Y, assuming he already has a few novels, a collection or two of verse, or perhaps some produced plays under his belt but has reached something of an artistic plateau. Two recent programs, both dedicated to giving established writers a wider berth of creative action, have already achieved a signal measure of success. Both, confusingly, bear the same initials

(APT), but both, clearly, have articulated specific and spirited objectives for themselves.

The first, the American Playwrights Theatre, was established as a nonprofit organization early in 1964. Its purpose was simply defined: to provide playwrights, in the words of David Ayers, the executive director of APT, "an alternative to Broadway, freedom from commercial restrictions, and a direct line to a national audience." For the American colleges and universities who would represent and supply the national audience, it would mean the opportunity to "present important premieres of new and major works by experienced playwrights and a repertoire of new plays unspoiled by the changes and subversions of an overly commercial New York theatre." Developed on the theory that an alliance of educational and community theatres could develop into the most important body of theatrical producers in America, APT went into operation with the clear intent of leading rather that following Broadway. Writing of the hardships encountered in persuading playwrights that their works would not be decimated by amateurs or lose their fresh bloom if tried out first by a group of universities, Ayers concludes (in the *Educational Theatre Journal* of October, 1965) that "when plays of thought and substance can find no Broadway production or can only struggle through a disastrously short run, the theatre suffers an inevitable decline in the creation of mature drama."

As a pilot project, the American Playwrights Theatre selected Robert Anderson's (author of *Tea and Sympathy*) *The Days Between,* a play dealing with a major crisis in the marital life of a teacher-writer. Its favorable reception by critics following its production at the Dallas Theater Center seemed to substantiate the purpose of APT and to promise an intensification of activity.

The second APT available to Older Writer Y is the American Place Theatre in New York City. It is here that non-theatre writers may find a theatrical forum for their conversion to the stage. In a program note for its first production late in 1964, the directorate of the American Place Theatre announced that it was in existence "to foster good writing for the theatre. It hopes to accomplish this by providing a place, a staff and a broad program of practical work to American writers of stature: our poets, novelists and philosophers who wish to use the dramatic form, and to serious playwrights." With the help of Ford and Rockefeller grants, the directors of APT set up shop in a building owned by the Protestant Episcopal Diocese on West 46th Street. A highly reputable poet, Robert Lowell, was the first to accept retreading into a playwright, with the opening of his *The Old Glory,* a tryptych of short plays relating to early American history, the American Place Theatre made an impressive start. Robert Lowell was followed by William Alfred, a Harvard professor, whose *Hogan's Goat,* a poetic genre picture of Irish immigrant life near the turn of the century, helped solidify the position of the American Place through supplying, by modest standards, a "hit."

What impact the American Place will have on men of letters is hard to estimate. The peculiar alchemy needed to transmute prose fiction into living theatre is uncertain at best; fundamental conceptions of human behavior must be radically altered before the novelist (working largely in the past tense) can begin to apprehend the vicious aesthetic squeeze he must put to his materials before ideas and characters can leap to life in the present tense. Poets and novelists may well be frightened off, unwilling to endure the strictures involved in drastically reducing large canvases to terse, vivid metaphors that scatter in front of an audience at a rapid clip.

Fortunately, the American Place Theatre has provided its own loophole. If the Place scares off or runs out of poets, novelists, and philosophers, it can always—as its credo promises—turn to "serious playwrights." Even more fortunate, however, is the very existence of the American Place and its enlightened leaders who are trying to refill a hitherto deadly vacuum. (It is significant, incidentally, to find the Episcopal church so involved in a theatre operation. The prospect of organized church institutions everywhere using their prestige, sanction, and resources to recultivate a need for the living theatre is most awesome. It will bear close watching in the next quarter century.)

In addition to the spread of regional professional theatres and the increased opportunities for alleviating the ordeal of the incipient playwright, there are still other firm signs of the new professionalism in the American theatre.

A distinguished attempt to bridge the gap between the university and the commercial theatre has met with unusual success at the University of Michigan. There, in 1962, two ostensibly incompatible ingredients were mixed together—an academically oriented University Theatre and a completely professional ensemble of actors, the Association of Producing Artists (APA). This hitherto unimaginable mixture has resulted, according to William P. Halstead, director of the University Theatre, in a "happy and rewarding" experience, even though a completely and mutually profitable means of integrating the two elements has not yet been discovered. In the meantime, the APA enjoys the relative serenity of a campus atmosphere in which to evolve and test its producing seasons before taking them to New York City, and the University of Michigan drama students profit from the exposure to and the association with the intensive artistic methods of a professional company.

There is much to commend this exchange of profits, the primary value being an inevitable modification of the insular roles played by the academic and the professional theatres. The arbitrary distinction that has often been drawn between what is "educational" and what is "commercial"—a distinction that presumably protects each party from being contaminated by the other—has been a stifling factor in the American theatre. As we will see shortly, university-taught drama, in order to "get respectable" has had to trim (if not cut off entirely) its professional nose to save its academic face. This has produced a form of cultural inbreeding that has been characterized by uneasy compromises in the development of drama curricula and by an inordinately defensive (if not blatantly apologetic) attitude on the part of curricula administrators. The representatives of the commercial theatre, on the other hand, rightly impatient with the circumlocutions of academic thinking and with the still present image of the fun-and-games amateur dramatic societies that developed in American universities in the early 1920's, felt no need to proselytize in the classroom.

What the amalgam of the University of Michigan and the APA most clearly suggests, however, is the long-delayed expression of a pivotal notion: to perpetrate a theatrical act automatically carries with it the responsibility *to be professional*. The ultimate objective of such an act may vary; i.e., to educate an audience, to train a group of actors, to give a playwright a hearing, to make money, to win a Critics' Circle prize, and so on. But there can be only one means to these ends: a total integration of the playwright's intent with the physical resources of the theatre, developed through a judicious use of the cerebral and emotional resources of the actor, for the purpose of a rich, coherent, and sustained form of dramatic communication. In other words, a *professional* performance.

Doctors, lawyers, and political chiefs are not trained to be amateurs, polite dilettantes, or members of an appreciative audience. They are trained to profess highly specialized crafts and to take considerable pride in the management of their skills. They are not necessarily dehumanized in the process; they are not required to suffer the stigma of unscholarly behavior; they are not less useful to society because they know and are good at their jobs.

Oddly, however, the graduate of most university drama departments emerges with a degree in vocational schizophrenia. He has been broadened by indulging in the liberal arts, humanized by exposure to some form of humanist tradition, indoctrinated with the particular educational bias of his professors, and prepared for a career by x number of hours in theatrical theory, history, and practice that constitute a "major." After four years of being alternately rounded and narrowed, the student is certainly likely to be pliant if not always professional.

A liberal education is valuable to any human being; it is paramount in the preparation of a theatre student, but only if it contributes to the creation of an enlightened craftsman, of an educated artist. Students of music, painting, and sculpture expect to receive, and are usually offered—with the full approval of university administrations—a program of study that enlarges the student's competence in his field. Students of theatre, however, are still made to bear the burden of Puritan-inspired skepticism about the value and substance of dramatic training and must, evidently, suffer the onus of semicompetence as expiation for all the former sins of "the profession."

I admit that the preceding observations have digressed slightly from identifying the "firm signs" of the new professionalism. The experiment at the University of Michigan, however, with its potential for reuniting at least two of the fragmented pieces of the American theatre, is most exciting. And if a national theatre, a theatre that strives to embrace and preserve the character and spirit of a dynamic people, is to emerge at all, the reuniting of the disparate elements of the American theatre around a hard core of educated professionals cannot happen soon enough.

Ironically, the university—that hotbed of cultural conservatism—has accomplished more in the way of fostering an American theatrical "tradition" and of developing a cadre of prospective professionals than any other single theatrical integer in America. And the university has done this without recourse to imitating foreign models. Indeed, with respect to the density and variety of theatre programs and courses, the American university is totally unique. With the possible exception of one or two British institutions, no other university system in the world can rival—or, for that matter, cares to rival—the comprehensive programs of theatre training available in the United States. According to the U.S. Office of Education, these programs now draw as many students as the fields of music and modern foreign languages, and more students than do other academic disciplines, such as journalism, earth science, and philosophy.

Generally unknown to the American public is the phenomenal growth of university drama. The statistics alone are impressive: a report on theatre in U.S. higher education (*Educational Theatre Journal,* May, 1964) indicates that upwards of 15,000 students are enrolled in almost 7,000 theatre courses in 900 accredited colleges and universities, and that nearly 100,000 undergraduates are involved each year in some form of play-producing activity. This head-count is bound to increase in view of the growth rate in instructional theatre programs of 20 per cent each year.

What is even more striking and more important than statistics or percentages are the special values that only a culturally conservative institution such as a university can propagate. Indeed, its conservatism—that often proclaimed handicap to the preparation of theatre professionals—is largely responsible for inculcating three major ideas into the growing numbers of students: first, that the inheritance of classical drama provides not only the intellectual satisfactions of reflecting on the living continuum of human vision but also a practical source of vivid theatre that should be exploited regularly and freely; second, that there are rational processes available—drawn from literature, science, and art—that can endow the theatre with a sense of coherence and purpose; and third, that effective and satisfying theatre depends heavily on a continuity of ideal and leadership.

So fundamental are these three ideas that they are rarely expressed any longer; they are simply *understood*. In fact, they seem to represent an intrinsic ethic of operation, virtually the only positive theatre ethic in operation at the moment either in the universities or out of them.

It would, of course, be silly to deny the fact that there are frequent abuses of this ethic; that some university theatres —and their directorates—are often more intent on image and empire-building than on substantiating the artistic basis of the drama; that there are fearful discrepancies between the seductive eloquence of catalog course descriptions and the way the courses are actually taught; and that instructional programs in theatre adopt awkward rationales in order to straddle the fence that separates the scholarly from the practical. But these are frailties of the flesh, not of the essential ethic.

Mortal inadequacies aside, this ethic represents the kind of uniform philosophy that is most essential to the character of a national theatre as well. It would not be too unrealistic, in fact, to suggest that the American university *is* America's national theatre. Viewed as a whole, the American university is an eminently successful repertory theatre, preserving and producing the works of the standard repertoire with a regularity that would be deeply pleasing to Sophocles, Shakespeare, or Ibsen. American universities, by their geographical dispersion, realize the "theatre centers" concept that has been attempted, unsuccessfully, by commercial producers. The universities possess some of the most commodious, tasteful, and well-equipped theatre plants in the world, enabling their theatre staffs to program seasons of complex and demanding works that would be unthinkable in a New York City legitimate playhouse. The American university, because of its four-year cycle of students, can most nearly approximate the ideal conditions for the development of ensemble acting styles and companies, an ideal that has been long cherished by theatre practitioners who have justifiably despaired over Broadway's inability to provide sustained training for actors. Finally, the American university enjoys the freedom to experiment with the drama, on whatever scale it chooses, unintimidated by the threat of box-office disasters or of the collapse of personal reputations.

The long-range significance of the university's new role will be substantial; its immediate impact on American culture is evident as college-trained actors, directors, and writers begin to assume major responsibilities in Broadway, Off-Broadway, and community theatres. Generally able to articulate critical standards, to crystallize ideas about the aesthetic ingredients of a dramatic presentation, and to preserve a healthy air of passionate skepticism toward the hysteria that often characterizes the imperfect art of play production, these former drama students constitute a new elite in the theatre who may, within the next quarter century, begin to dominate all facets of the amateur and commercial stage.

If we pause for an interim reckoning of firm signs of a new professionalism in the American theatre, we find an impressive tally: the spread of regional professional theatres that seem to be taking root, the increased opportunities for playwrights to find a sympathetic ear and an available stage, the experimental conjunction of commercial and academic enterprises, and the unexpected new role for American universities as a credible framework for a national theatre.

There is one other firm sign. It has been reserved for last in this category because it appears, superficially, to be the least defensible as a positive and useful token of anything: the Broadway musical. To me, it is one of the most encouraging signs of all. Never mind America's legendary "genius" for musical comedy; never mind our long tradition of musical theatre that developed out of *Flora, or Hob in the Well* (1734–35), out of that clumsy—though overwhelmingly popular—ballet-melodrama *The Black Crook* (1866), out of *Show Boat* (1928), *Oklahoma* (1943) or *West Side Story* (1957); never mind the escapist, theatre party or expense account philosophies that seem to undergird the popularity of the musical, philosophies that are sustained by sentimental melodies, seminude girls, and smashing finales. Our talent for, history of, and attitudes toward the musical have been well and widely documented.

I suspect, however, that the musical theatre represents something more than an antidote to an oppressive life or a celebration of artful tunesmiths. Despite the dreadful frequency of derivative, unmelodious, and tasteless musicals, the form offers special satisfactions which unfortunately are not common enough in the theatre.

For one thing, musical theatre is *complete* theatre. Its attempt to synthesize dramatic idea and melodic expression raises the form to the nearest thing to a 20th-century poetic theatre. A palatable poetry, to be sure, but wholly appropriate to the casual, intimate, and unsophisticated contemporary social attitudes and idioms of speech. The phenomenon of "total theatre" that the musical represents is based on a relatively familiar notion: up to a certain emotional level, language alone can sustain the dramatic metaphor; beyond a certain level—during extremely ecstatic or depressive states—language betrays the metaphor by being unequal to it. (We have all noted, I'm sure, the utter banality of dialogue and lyrics of much grand opera; the cosmic passions these words are striving to describe would shrivel without the lyric dimension supplied by the music.)

The musical theatre, then, provides the inevitable extension of prosaic words and ideas. And in a world strangled by prosaic communications, the musical has rightly earned its popularity by providing an approachable conception of poetry: the intensification of experience by a dramatic narration raised to a second or third power by the melody and cadence of song.

Another aspect of the musical's total theatre experience—and one which most legitimate dramas seem to have forgotten—is its commitment to a primarily sensual demonstration of dramatic ideas. In other words, a visceral and neural theatre, freely and unashamedly paying tribute to the sentient rather than cerebral nature of man. The musical has undeservedly been classified as a "lower order" of mammal because of the nature of its appeal: sentimental, energetic, and colorful. And yet these are the very traits that are so noticeably and sorely missing from nonmusical drama, traits that the 20th-century theatre has stamped out with the moral vigor of a puritanical schoolmarm.

There remains, however, a real longing, a persistent yearning for sensory spectacle in the theatre, a yen for opportunities to stretch the sentimental muscle, to work out the intellectual kinks that develop in a seemingly joyless world. What the legitimate, "serious" theatre has taken away, the musical returns in full measure: the joy of being alive.

In sum, I suspect that a major reason for the enthusiastic support that contemporary audiences give to musicals devolves upon the musical's singular capacity to affirm rather than deny life. This is not only a pleasant antidote to the ponderous nay-sayers of the drama, but an essential one. The support also bespeaks the refusal of American audiences to surrender their dramatic birthright.

In view of the civilizing spread of regional theatres, the new channels opening for playwrights, the friendly welcome given to professional repertory theatre on the university campus, the potent new role of the academic theatre, and the vitality of the American musical theatre, the prospect of Tinker Bell's appearance begins to seem hopeful indeed. Even the emergence of an American Theatre begins to be less remote.

But these firm signs are still not enough to bring about a realization of these prospects. Weak signs still await straightening. There are at least two other types of dramatic activity in the United States that have not yet been fully admitted to the magic circle of full public support and understanding: children's theatre and community theatre. The position they hold is considerably weaker than it should be, and this weakness threatens the firm signs of a new professionalism. To ignore or downgrade theatre for children is to deny potential audience—and thus a major taste-making force— before it gets the chance to *become* an audience. To dismiss or be patronizing toward community theatre is to threaten one of the more civilizing features of civic life.

Popular conceptions of children's theatre are as varied as they are wrong. "Kiddies' shows," even among professionals who should know better, have not been able to shake off the overtones of preciosity and naïveté, overtones that are totally incompatible with the revelations of psychologists and child guidance experts. Indeed, the gap that exists between what we know about the emotional needs and growth patterns of children and the quality of plays and productions that are offered to children is alarming. The inspirational remarks by spokesmen for the national Children's Theatre Conference—a division of the American

Educational Theatre Association—notwithstanding, children's theatre in America continues to be associated with (1) worthy programs of culturally minded social and educational organizations (Junior Leagues, PTA's) that are eager to "do something better" for youngsters—although many of the organizations would be hard pressed to identify the precise nature of the "something," or why it is "better"; (2) programs of social adjustment or improvement in which theatrical activity contributes to language skills, health habits, and poise, and otherwise assists the shy or sensitive child through rough periods in his or her life; (3) prancing fairies, animate flowers, and pretty princesses, all looking vaguely medieval; (4) quick, conscience-salving jolts of culture by which parents discharge their moral duty to their children; (5) making money, a practice which children's theatre especially enjoys.

It's a curious thing. Of all the European theatre traditions we have adopted, borrowed, or stolen, the one we have left virtually untouched is one of the most vigorous of all: the European tradition of children's entertainments. The century-old practice of Christmas pantomimes, marionettes, Punch and Judy shows, one-ring circuses, the legendary pranks of Tyl Eulenspiegel, and the festivals of storytelling, dance, and song seem to have eluded us. With such a regular diet of classical and traditional entertainments for children, the role of the child is dignified by being regularly allotted a share of local culture. Could this be, at least in part, the origin of local and national pride?

American children's theatre has not begun to sense its own might, its own potential for altering the theatrical axis of the country, because it has not probed deeply enough into the peculiar nature of the child who comes to see the play; nor has it articulated fully enough the transcendent objectives in putting on the play in the first place. In other words, children's theatre has not yet assumed a major role in the formulation and pursuit of American cultural aspirations.

If I may so presume, I will suggest something about the nature of the child and the scope of the objectives. This will be done less in the interests of psychological science than in the instruction of adults who remain, for the most part, resolutely opaque about the probable connection between an impoverished adult theatre and an underdeveloped child theatre.

In recent years, we have come to considerable knowledge about the interests and psychological needs of the child. The knowledge is startling for the most part because it's old knowledge, cultural and racial intuition, origin-and-growth-of-the-species stuff. Objective studies and measurements, however, have validated the old knowledge so that we can now make relevant some of the long familiar platitudes.

Chief among these platitudes is the notion that children are, as a rule, sensuous and compulsive creatures, both imploding and exploding with largely undirected energies, tensions, and vivid imaginations. Both the real and illusory impressions that impinge on children from the world around them strike them at a clip faster than they can assimilate, intensifying all their energies and tensions. All those ennobling ethical and moral codes that characterize the civilized and adult person are, in general, totally alien to the child because all ethical and moral systems are not translated into those dynamic signals, those sensory impressions that a child may interpret and absorb into his own being. In other words, only a very tenuous bridge exists between the so-called rational processes of the adult world and the essentially irrational behavior of the junior world.

A second platitude is the fact that children are abstract thinkers, professional symbolists; indeed, they have to be as an act of self-defense. With so many stimuli activating the emotional and physical nature of the child and with so few logic skills to sort and compute them, the child is obliged to modify and reduce those stimuli to their most revealing, stark, and useful state. Any picture drawn by a child quickly demonstrates the young artist's necessary aptitude for abstractions and symbols.

Now combine platitudes: the steady, in-and-out flow of strong sensory impulses and the natural propensity for rendering experience into its boldest outlines leads us to rediscover the natural relationship between the life of the child and the function of the artist. This relationship is neither accidental nor forced; it exists.

If the child, like the artist, responds best to those life experiences that *most nearly rival* the intense sensory-symbolic activity that goes on regularly within him, then the theatre's power—derived from intense sense-and-symbol representations of life—to direct social behavior is enormous. Certainly the theatre can exert more influence than tableaux-ridden, superciliously moral, and grossly cute child drama would suggest.

Yet for all its patronizing and conscientious airs, adult society has underrated the natural compatibility that exists between children and the theatre and has thus denied itself a potent instrument for inculcating firm and lasting cultural ideals. If it is important that society transmit "messages" relating to moral standards, to racial myth or national lore, let the messages be transmitted joyously. Let a genuine communion take place: if the child naturally turns to movement, color, dream, mimicry, fantasy, symbol, and conflict as unconscious devices to bring about a resolution of the raw and vital impulses that swirl through him; and if the theatre naturally employs—as it must—movement, color, dream, mimicry, fantasy, symbol, and conflict as conscious devices to bring about a resolution of artistic problems, let the theatre's methods of resolving a human crisis be fully applied, in an exemplary manner, to the unformed impulses of the child. Not to squelch these impulses, but to refine and dignify them.

So what have "kiddies' shows" got to do with the American theatre? No conception of an American Theatre can be formulated until it begins at the beginning. There is no beginning better than children.

Some small progress has been made toward pointing out the proper beginnings. Writers on children's theatre, such as Winifred Ward and Geraldine Brain Siks, have brightened some dark corners, and the Children's Theatre Conference has approved an "operating code" that outlines sensible objectives for children's theatre. A few regional theatres for children—notably in Portland, Maine; Nashville, Tennessee; Kansas City, Kansas; and elsewhere— have devoted themselves to the problems of a vital engagement with the child mind and spirit. But it is not enough.

A similar deficiency—our second weak sign—exists in the amateur community theatres across the country. Here the problem is not social adjustment or sensory refinement, but rather cultural identity and civic responsibility. In short, the community theatre phenomenon in the United States appears to be suffering from acute image damage.

This wasn't always the case. In the first two decades of the 20th century, community—or "Little"—theatres were formidable and righteous combatants against the artistic bleakness of the commercial stage. The wave of the "New Drama" was reaching American shores; plays by Ibsen, Chekov, Strindberg, and Shaw—a body of drama that was shortly to become the classic literature of the 20th-century theatre—was cold-shouldered by commercial producers and left homeless in a foreign country. As a gesture of cultural hospitality and artistic conscience, intrepid Little Theatres made room for the visitors at the Little Theatre in Chicago, at the Toy Theatre in Boston, at Plays and

Players in Philadelphia, and at the most successful little theatre of all, the Washington Square Players (later to become The Theatre Guild).

Their objectives were clear and honorable: to counteract the hostility of Broadway by creating independent theatres and to spread the good word about the new breed of serious dramatists who were revolutionizing the European theatre.

These early *avant garde* producers adopted more than the playwrights; the total conception of an independent theatre movement was inspired by the *Theatre Libre* in Paris, the *Freie Bühne* in London—all of which were dedicated to breaking economic shackles and experimenting freely with fresh dramatic visions.

American manifestations of this lofty philosophy were, unhappily, short lived. As the shock of the "new" drama wore off, risky foreign plays began to seem economically feasible, and commercial managers started making playhouses available to these now not-so-oddball playwrights.

Image Number One of community theatre faded out.

Having lost its sense of mission, its aura of combat for the great good cause, the community theatre, in the late 1920's and early 1930's, found itself in a perilous vacuum. What banner shall be raised now? An obvious banner; one that had been waving sporadically and weakly over the American theatre for two hundred years: the quest for Culture. It was a pretentious banner, to be sure, but hardly unjustified. Indeed, by refocusing its energies, the community theatre sought to repair the damage to the broken continuity that once existed between art and life.

The energies were dissipated quickly. For all its eloquent motives, the community theatre movement fell into the waiting hands of erstwhile amateur actors, ingenuous matrons and clubwomen, and zealous businessmen who believed, somehow, that selling plumbing supplies had a natural kinship with selling theatre. I mean no disrespect to local amateurs, matrons, or plumbing salesmen; but what was once a professionally oriented program devoted to breaching the walls of a grimly unimaginative theatre, degenerated—by the middle 1930's—into an inadvertently fatuous, artistically inept enterprise that reawakened all the negative overtones of the word "amateur." Bearing the torch for high culture is a noble thing, George Kelley implies in his play about Little Theatres (appropriately titled *The Torch-Bearers*), providing that the audience doesn't notice that your scenery has fallen down.

Image Number Two of community theatre faded out.

Image Number Three began to take shape briskly, if uncertainly, in the years immediately following World War II. No longer professional (except in aspiration) and much chastened by its failure to reinstate High Culture to a proper throne, the community theatre more sensibly adopted the role of crucible for local social and artistic energies. This was not an especially easy role. To be, at one and the same time, a center for communal and casual good fellowship ("We'll have a lot of fun") and an arena for severe artistic principles and disciplines invites dangers of the most fundamental kind. Not the least of these dangers is an inevitable ambiguity of purpose that confuses the sociability-seekers (who would rather prattle than paint) and alarms the serious *artistes* (who would, of course, rather study than socialize).

Because of the impossibly vulnerable and frustrating position in which a dual purpose community theatre finds itself—an elite and exclusive art form floundering in a sea of democratic and all-inclusive operating principles—it does not, as a rule, possess the strength to become a dominant symbol of a community's character or to invade, on a more intimate level, the lives and actions of a community's citizens. As a result, the community theatre is still woefully lacking in support—moral, physical, and economic. City X will set aside "Days," "Weeks," and sometimes "Months" to celebrate flower festivals, local baseball teams, industrial development drives, animal charities, and regional historical sites, but it will seldom find an "Hour" to extol local theatre amateurs. City X is partly at fault for failing to acknowledge artistic effort as a major community resource; the city then compounds the failure by failing to offer responsible civic guidance. (Art councils, funded by state legislatures, have had to come into existence to draw up the cultural slack left by the individual municipalities.) But X Community Theatre is partly at fault too for not having forged a working principle out of the two seemingly antithetical elements—democratic license and artistic restraint; for not having formulated *first* a policy to provide a sturdy continuity of leadership (artistic and administrative) and *then* programing seasons; for not having made its resources and services consistently available to all those civic agencies (social, medical, mental, and religious) that are already established symbols of a community's intrinsic responsibility to its own citizenry; and for not having resisted the temptation to be "Little Broadways," a role that can never be satisfactorily achieved in the face of uneven amateur talent, of the eagerness of Hollywood to transform Broadway hits into slick motion pictures, or the accessibility to professional road companies and summer stock.

Despite the community theatre's inability to find the kind of distinctive identity for itself that emanates from a clear philosophic vision of how an Elevated Art can survive at a Grassroots Level, such a theatre conception remains the most feasible approach to the most pressing dilemma of contemporary culture: how to restore the natural integration of art and life.

Perhaps this integration is nothing more than a myth, a

delightful fantasy that naïve critics, like myself, hope to propagate. Perhaps it's necessary to rediscover the natural integration among the various arts themselves first, and then try to reweave them into the fabric of enlightened everyday mortal experience. A step must be taken somewhere, however; at some point the continuing atomizing of the arts must be challenged and an alternative proposed.

Community theatre could not exist—indeed, no theatre at all could exist—if the creative act of the artistic recreation of life did not offer profound satisfactions to those who are either immediately involved in the act or to those who are largely witnesses of it. It is a primitive act, to be sure, calling for the transforming of an ephemeral spirit (the dramatic theme or idea, the metaphor of character as a combination of internal and external experience) into a solid substance (the performance itself, the concrete modifications of perception on the part of both player and spectator). The immediate effect of such a transformation is, of course, the tangible pleasure of having dealt cogently and artfully with largely intangible materials. The long-range effect, however, is more important: having been touched by the theatre, by its capacity for both enlarging human actions and distilling human beliefs, the participant must, perforce, be different. He is now more sensitized to the infinite possibilities of human actions and beliefs, more facile in abstracting them into symbolic expressions of human behavior, and more eager to embody these symbols in dramatic terms. He is, in other words, beginning to experience a reintegration of human experience and artistic form and to certify, as a personal ethic, the immutability of this integration.

It would be ridiculous, of course, to suggest that community theatre need merely throw a switch and such an integration will suddenly occur. No such thing. The fact that community theatre is, however, still in the market for an operational ethic, one that might serve as a matrix for its opposing objectives, makes the notion of a strengthened culture through the vital reintegration of art and life especially inviting. This, I submit, is the still unmaterialized Image Number 3 of community theatre.

The appearance of Tinker Bell as a token of the first beginnings of an American Theatre now seems feasible. The stimulating new professionalism evident in the regional and university theatre, the surprisingly healthy commitment to developing new playwrights, and the vital cultural force implicit in children's and community theatre may soon dispel the generally gloomy image of a vacant and timid national theatre.

There is one other set of indicators—four so-called *anti* signs—that may, more than any other symptoms of change and improvement, achieve more lasting results. The four *anti* signs manifest themselves in current theatrical movements: the Method School approach to acting, the Theatre of the Absurd, the Theatre of Cruelty, and "Happenings." That they are designated *"anti"* suggests, rightly, a robust artistic arrogance toward the invalid values and practices of the contemporary stage and a conscious effort to disrupt virtually all the placid tenets of rationality in art. All four manifestations emerge from a uniquely 20th-century phenomenon: an attack on the fundamental philosophy of the theatre and its function as a cultural barometer of its society.

That the attack is real is clear enough; that it has taken many forms in encouraging enough; that these forms have increased in frequency and tempo in the past fifteen to twenty years is the most promising event of all. The specific manifestations of the attack, what each has set out to accomplish, and what all share as a common vision of the theatre's destiny deserve at least a brief overview. No attempt will be made to put them in chronological order because of their currency and overlap; besides, each manifestation originated, ideologically, at different times during the late 19th and early 20th centuries but came to fruition almost simultaneously in the middle of the present century.

Manifestation Number One: the Method School of Acting. An unpleasant and inaccurate image clings to the Method Actor and to his shrine, The Actors Studio: the T-shirted, armpit-rubbing, mumbling performer who tediously stokes up his emotional furnace in the hope of warming his senses, his memory, and his psyche. The Method does, of course, call for an intensive exploration of the interior designs and motives for human behavior, much after the manner of actor training postulated by Constantin Stanislavski, the Moscow Art Theatre's celebrated proponent of a meticulous realism in performance. Where the trouble—and the inaccurate image—arises is in the simple failure of some Studio-trained American actors to employ the method as a *preparatory* rather than a performance instrument, to confuse the search for vital and personal imagery with the demonstration of the results of the search.

Despite this inevitable limitation, the Method School remains true to the character of a "revolutionary" movement: an uneasy blend of impatience and hope tenuously embodied in a group of working principles. The Method's impatience is with the parasitic residue of a classical acting style, a style that ranks exterior form over interior experience and that replaces legitimacy and immediacy of feeling with a too facile body of biomechanical technique. The Method's hope is for a return to the primal sources of personal behavior; to those organic impulses that lie deep in the racial experience and memory of each human being, impulses that constitute the natural substructure of all human actions; and to a body of performance systems that are free of cant, of pat formulas, of predictable posturing; systems that are, instead, inevitable symbols of the ostensibly profound resonances that occur within the role (and thus within the actor, and thus within the man, and thus within life itself).

Manifestation Number Two: the Theatre of the Absurd. For slightly less than ten years—from the early 1950's to the early 1960's—the Absurdists were the true and agonized spokesmen for Alienated Man. Samuel Beckett, Eugène Ionesco, Jean Genet, and Edward Albee, among others, prophesied—in caustic, studiously banal, and rationally inchoate images of man—the total collapse of all human value. From the lunatic parody of procreation in Ionesco's *The Future is in Eggs,* to the mordant futility of Beckett's *Waiting for Godot,* to the passionate psychosis of Genet's *The Maids,* the Theatre of the Absurd challenged the vacuity of contemporary writing and producing modes while underscoring the singularly perilous and eternal conditions of man as an absurd and irrational creature.

Both the challenging and the underscoring were eminently healthy and necessary activities. In the challenge, however, lay an artistic contradiction that could not be resolved by the professional Absurdists and that finally undid them: a rational form of communication (i.e., the theatre) will never completely submit to a wholly irrational view of life (i.e., Absurdity). Despite how formless, disjointed, mechanical, and ambiguous life may have become, to deliver a "message" to this effect requires at least the rudiments of clear form. An audience still must be told in articulate terms that an audience is made up of people incapable of articulating the philosophic premises which guide their lives.

By underscoring the innately absurd nature of man, the Absurdists merely crystallized the 20th century's version of a universal dilemma: man is inexorably alone, vulnerable, and frightened; he is fearful of a commitment to the usual ethical codes (social, religious, or moral) because these codes have too often betrayed him, yet he finds intolerable the distinct sense of drift that pervades all his actions. He wishes desperately to be involved in the making of those moral judgments that give shape to his society, yet he finds that he has contributed to the making of an impersonal society that cares nothing for his wishes.

To see life as it really is, to undertake—as Jean Paul Sartre makes Orestes in *The Flies* undertake—a "trip downward" to encounter all the frustrations and terrors of existence, to live life, in other words, existentially is one thing; to attempt to capture and record in dramatic form the complexities of this downward trip is quite another. At least one reason for the short, unhappy life of the Theatre of the Absurd was that it was too successful as theatre, skillfully reducing the complexities of absurdism to those topical features an audience would most readily grasp: caricature, parody, repetition, humor, and physical violence. The Absurdists, in other words, were much too good as entertainers to be generally very pervasive as instruments for social change.

The Theatre of the Absurd is now a dead issue; and if it didn't entirely houseclean the theatre or tidy up problems of noncommunication, noncommitment, or alienation, it showed us what brooms to use.

Manifestation Number Three: the Theatre of Cruelty. If the Method School of Acting was out to nullify the arbitrariness of a lingering classical ideal in the theatre, and if the Theatre of the Absurd was dedicated to eschewing the philosophical mud that was coating human values and encrusting the theatre, the Theatre of Cruelty chose as its target the whole nerveless, flaccid, unprovocative realistic stage. So helplessly entrenched was this stage and so utterly untouched by the sweeping social and artistic currents of the 20th century, an approach to theatrical production was needed that could, by sensually violent means, drive the play and the spectator into a shocking confrontation with one another. This was to be the nature of theatrical Cruelty.

In a collection of essays (*The Theatre and Its Double*) he composed in the early 1930's, Antonin Artaud—actor, producer, visionary, and occasional madman—proclaimed that the theatre had lost its "appetite for life," that it had been victimized by the "misdeeds of the psychological theatre," and that only the rediscovery of a dramatic form of "all nerves and heart" could restore the kind of emotional magnitude that makes the theatre a necessity rather than a handicap.

To reassert its necessity, Artaud argued, the theatre would have to be reendowed with "everything that is in crime, love, war, or madness" by concentrating on dramas of famous personages, of spectacle, of superhuman devotions, and the sense of cataclysmic struggle that once propelled the old myths into existence. To be precise, it would have to be a theatre of concrete bite, involving all necessary acts of emotional intimidation to force the spectator into a more total engagement with the reality of his own existence than he ever experienced before. (With the production of *Marat/Sade,* thirty years after the publication of *The Theatre and Its Double,* the Theatre of Cruelty would at last find a home.)

Eager to combat the fatigue of the human organs, Artaud would have the theatre explode with visual and aural images that assault the spectator from all sides, forcing an escalation of his emotions until they are fully equal to the barrage of images that are being hurled at him: cries, groans, apparitions, surprise, the magic beauty of costumes; resplendent lighting and the incantational beauty of voices, the charms of harmony, rare notes of music, the colors of objects; masks, effigies yards high, and sudden changes of light that arouse sensations of heat and cold.

If the conventional stage and auditorium interfere with

this sensory onslaught, then abolish them. A site without partitions or barriers will do instead; a hangar or barn will do, so long as there is direct, unimpeded communication between actor and spectator, both of whom are engulfed by the action of the play.

If the written text of the play interferes with the action, then abolish the play. "We shall not act a written play," Artaud insists, "but we shall make attempts at direct staging, around themes, facts, and known works. . . . There is no theme, however vast, that can be denied us."

The primeval echoes in the theories of Artaud are clear enough; so are the echoes of Dionysian revels of Ancient Greece, of Titanic clashes, of human pain, of magic, and of the peculiarly revitalizing experience of having the five senses stretched to the limit of their endurance.

Against the background of contemporary stage practice, Artaud's vision of the theatre's function seems singularly mad and dangerous. It is neither; an *old* vision, perhaps, and an elusive one, but utterly rational and beneficial. To generate only *half* the emotional energy of a dramatic idea is to cheat the spectator and emasculate the theatre; both are enfeebled; both are satisfied with disguises and demi-truths; and both, finally, atrophy, like a disabled arm, until the original function is lost. Artaud's vision, then, is violent therapy.

Manifestation Number Four: "Happenings." Perhaps the reader has already detected a progression implicit in the first three manifestations of attack on the 20th-century theatre. The Method School of Acting was characterized by disenchantment; the Theatre of the Absurd by despair; the Theatre of Cruelty by violence. The direction, clearly, is toward psychological disorientation and artistic chaos. The threat of an anti- or non-art has been, like a Damoclean sword, raised over the theatre whenever either Reason or Feeling, or both at the same time, have been held suspect. In view of the Dada aspect of Happenings, I suppose we will have to assume that the sword is again raised over the 20th century, that reason and feeling have been completely routed, and that we are uncomfortably close to the point on the artistic spectrum marked "Every Man for Himself."

A Happening is an event, entirely random in nature, that may occur singly or in concert with other events. No conscious plan controls these events, each participant being responsible for whatever the accident of personal impulse may lead him to do. Objects are freely used and may or may not have any relationship to the person using the object or to any other object nearby. A Happening begins at a more or less specific time, may confine itself to a single location, or may crop up anywhere in the theatre, in the building or in the city. Having freed themselves from the old-fashioned inhibitions of story, plot, character, and action, Happenings are not obliged to be coherent, structured, human, or dynamic. Indeed, a Happening will play down these traits on the premise (we must assume this premise since it would be utterly inconsistent for a Happening-maker to resort to logic to explain his function) that the worldwide absence of traditional human values has created a void in which the humanist platitudes about form, logic, and purpose make no sense.

A participant in a Happening will surrender completely, as if under the influence of a strong narcotic, to whatever strikes his fancy at the moment. He may sit in a bathtub, fully clothed, and weep; he may remove his clothing; he may turn radios on and off incessantly; he may sit on the third rung of a ladder and shout obscenities at the audience; he may float on a rubber raft in a Manhattan pool.

There are strong and clear overtones of both Absurdity and Cruelty in Happenings. The absurd is evident in the total destruction of all rational processes and the consciously inflicted injury to the perceptions of an audience. Indeed, Happenings seem to be not only an amalgam of its two more popular brethren but a final step toward the obliteration of conscious artistry in the theatre.

On a purely philosophic basis, Happenings must, unfortunately, be taken seriously. The concept of the monumental nothingness of life that the Happening depicts has just enough validity to make disconnected events seem entirely credible. What makes Happenings frivolous, however, stems from this same philosophy; if life is meaningless, if existence is nothingness, and if value is pointless, to perform a Happening is, theoretically, redundant. It may produce, perhaps, a form of emotional placation for the performer of the "event," but a true void can only be surrounded, not filled. To claim that a living mortal—a familiar container for intellectual and biological processes—can so completely dehumanize himself as to perpetrate senseless, machinelike acts results *not* in a pretentious "message about our times" but in a fundamental contradiction of intention and method. It is this contradiction that becomes the "message" to an audience, a message of tension that produces discomfiture, laughter, and—ultimately—retreat from whatever it is that is Happening.

There is a peculiar equation a theatre audience applies that Happenings-makers seem to forget: the more radical is the departure from familiar human practices and beliefs the more diligently the audience will "fill in the gaps," avidly reconstituting the missing parts in order to restore a semblance of order to the proceedings. Shock techniques won't alter this equation because the quest for order is deep enough in the human marrow to resist the shocks.

Thus, Happenings have only interim value, pronouncing their own death sentence with every random event presented. What will finally make Happenings succumb to what John Simon (writing in the Sunday *New York Times* recently) called "moral abulia and intellectual aphasia" is its self-indulgent, adolescent, insular, and accidental mode of operation. Above all, Happenings will fail because they are more satisfied to merely report on the bleakness of contemporary society than to use whatever talents and imaginations are involved to lead the society toward a reasonable alternative to its bleakness.

All four of what I have termed the *anti* signs may be viewed, on a larger scale, as laments for the frightening schism that has developed in this century between the traditional manifestations of life and the aesthetic imperatives of art. In their efforts to close the schism, the *anti* sign manufacturers have celebrated the notion of chance (Happenings), have encouraged a veritable rape of the senses (Theatre of Cruelty), have painted grim pictures of alienation (Theatre of the Absurd), and have abolished the glib certitudes of human behavior (the Method). Philosophically, each seems to have a different target; practically, each has developed an intrinsically different methodology. What binds the four *anti* signs together is their massive attack on the efficacy of traditional art forms (a periodic necessity) and, indeed, on the probability that *any* man-made artistic product can capture and preserve the violently shifting attitudes of the 20th century. Predictably, however, the attack is two-edged; the necessary ambivalence that is basic to any self-proclaimed revolutionary clique is very much in evidence. The spokesmen for the *anti* signs all wish to destroy as well as create: to destroy proscenium arches in favor of the dream of free, unencumbered space; to destroy the dormant audience in favor of the dream of totally committed, actively engaged, and sensorially heightened spectators; to destroy the analytically tidy, carbon-copied realism of the modern stage in favor of a freshly perceived vision of reality; to destroy the sophistic humbug and quasi-intellectual cant that has incarcerated the theatre in favor of a visionary language that will restore vitality and imagination to the theatre.

The four *anti* signs, furthermore, are devoutly polemical. They have lessons to teach—moral, artistic, and social— and they are determined to impress the lessons on their pupils. Audiences (i.e., the American public) must be shown that there are aesthetic options that they have been ignoring; that there are dimensions of human frailty as yet unobserved; that the so-called "science" of playcraft or play production is so profoundly vulnerable that it must be continually reexamined and defended; and that the theatre— as one of the most eminent of the humanist traditions— must be recreated every time a child is born or else the leavening process of human growth will be threatened by all the marauding interests of commercial depravity.

Like explosions on the surface of the sun, this century's crop of *anti* signs may shortly subside. They will leave a residue of beliefs and practices in the atmosphere, an altered structure of aesthetic matter that will settle on all those who come during or after.

In sum, the incidence and especially the frequency of these *anti* signs, their boldness in taking on perplexing philosophical issues, and the urgency with which they formulate and sell their theories suggest an approaching climax in the changeling life of the American theatre.

Tinker Bell may yet be born in the 20th century. From a broad geographical base of professional regional and university theatres, a sensible structure of opportunities for serious playwrights, and a potential strengthening of artistic perceptions through amateur, community, and children's theatre, Tinker Bell may find a sturdy home waiting. Not even the iconoclasm of the *anti* sign visionaries will drive her away; indeed, all they have been trying to do is to knock down the obstacles in her path.

The emergence of an American Theatre has become a legitimate possibility.

Suggested Reading

The following books and articles proved invaluable both as general background on the contemporary theatre and as sources of the specific theory and practice that best characterize the climate of the 20th century.

BOOKS

Artaud, Antonin. *The Theater and its Double.* New York: Grove Press, 1958.

Bentley, Eric. *The Playwright as Thinker.* New York: Harcourt, Brace & Company, Inc., 1946.

Bogard and Oliver (eds.). *Modern Drama—Essays in Criticism.* New York: Oxford University Press, 1965.

Brousard, Louis. *American Drama: Contemporary Allegory from Eugene O'Neill to Tennessee Williams.* Norman: University of Oklahoma Press, 1962.

Brustein, Robert. *The Theatre of Revolt.* Boston: Little, Brown & Company, 1964.

———. *Seasons of Discontent.* New York: Simon and Schuster, 1965.

Clark, Barrett. *Eugene O'Neill: The Man and His Plays.* New York: Dover Publications, Inc., 1947.

Clurman, Harold. *Lies Like Truth.* New York: Grove Press, 1960.

Corrigan, Robert (ed.). *Theatre in the Twentieth Century.* New York: Grove Press, Inc., 1965.

Downer, Alan. *Fifty Years of American Drama 1900–1950.* Chicago: Henry Regnery Company, 1951.

Esslin, Martin. *The Theatre of the Absurd*. New York: Double-day & Company, Inc., 1961.

Fergusson, Francis. *The Human Image in Dramatic Literature*. New York: Doubleday & Company, Inc., 1957.

Flanagan, Hallie. *Arena*. New York: Duell, Sloan & Pearce, Inc., 1940.

Flexner, Eleanor. *American Playwrights: 1918–1938*. New York: Simon and Schuster, Inc., 1938.

Frenz, Horst (ed.). *American Playwrights on Drama*. New York: Hill and Wang, 1965.

Gassner, John. *Masters of the Drama*. New York: Random House, 1940.

Gelb, Barbara and Arthur. *O'Neill*. New York: Delta Books, 1964.

Hart, Moss. *Act One*. New York: The New American Library, 1960.

Hewitt, Barnard. *Theatre U.S.A. 1668–1957*. New York: McGraw-Hill Book Company, Inc., 1959.

Jones, Robert Edmond. *The Dramatic Imagination*. New York: Duell, Sloan & Pearce, 1941.

Krutch, Joseph Wood. *The American Drama Since 1918*. New York: George Braziller, Inc., 1957.

Lewis, Allan. *American Plays and Playwrights of the Contemporary Theatre*. New York: Crown Publishers, 1965.

McCarthy, Mary. *Sights and Spectacles 1937–1956*. New York: Farrar, Straus and Cudahy, 1956.

Miller, Jordan Y. *American Dramatic Literature*. New York: McGraw-Hill Book Company, Inc., 1961.

Nelson, Benjamin. *Tennessee Williams: The Man and His Work*. New York: Ivan Obolensky, Inc., 1961.

Peacock, Ronald. *The Poet in the Theatre*. New York: Hill and Wang, 1960.

Quinn, Arthur Hobson. *Representative American Plays*. New York: Appleton-Century-Crofts, Inc., 1957.

Rice, Elmer. *The Living Theatre*. New York: Harper and Brothers, 1959.

Taubman, Howard. *The Making of the American Theatre*. New York: Coward McCann, Inc., 1965.

Tischler, Nancy. *Tennessee Williams: Rebellious Puritan*. New York: Citadel Press, 1961.

Weales, Gerald. *American Drama Since World War II*. New York: Harcourt, Brace & World, Inc., 1962.

Young, Stark. *Immortal Shadows*. New York: Charles Scribner's Sons, 1948.

ARTICLES

"After the Fall: Arthur Miller's Return," *Newsweek,* Feb. 3, 1964.

"The Angel of the Odd," *Time* (March 9, 1962).

Ayers, David H. "American Playwrights Theatre—A Progress Report," *Educational Theatre Journal,* Vol. XVII (October, 1965).

Brustein, Robert. "Arthur Miller's Mea Culpa," *New Republic,* February 8, 1964.

Clurman, Harold. "The Old Glory," *The Nation,* Vol. 199 (November 23, 1964).

Couchman, Gordon W. "Arthur Miller's Tragedy of Babbit," *Educational Theatre Journal,* Vol. VII (1955).

Dukore, Bernard (ed.). "Professional Companies, Professionalism, and the University Theatre Department: A Symposium," *Educational Theatre Journal,* Vol. XVIII (May, 1966).

Hobgood, Burnet M. "Theatre in U.S. Higher Education: Emerging Patterns and Problems," *Educational Theatre Journal,* Vol. XVI (May, 1964).

Jackson, Esther M. "The Emergence of the Anti-Hero in the Contemporary Drama," *Central States Speech Journal,* Vol. XII (Winter, 1961).

Kernodle, George R. "The Death of the Little Man," *Carleton Drama Bulletin* (May, 1952).

"The Miller's Tale," *Time* (January 31, 1964).

Moss, Leonard. "Biographical & Literary Allusion in *After the Fall,*" *Educational Theatre Journal* (March, 1966).